Benjamin Franklin Tillinghast

**Rock Island Arsenal, in Peace and in War**

Benjamin Franklin Tillinghast

**Rock Island Arsenal, in Peace and in War**

ISBN/EAN: 9783744718523

Printed in Europe, USA, Canada, Australia, Japan

Cover: Foto ©ninafisch / pixelio.de

More available books at **www.hansebooks.com**

MOLINE WAGON CO. MOLINE ILL.

OFFICE

MOLINE

THE
MOLINE

The Genuine Moline FARM FREIGHT AND SPRING WAGONS.

LIGHT RUNNING AND DURABLE

i

ii

F. H. GRIGGS, President.
ROBERT KRAUSE, Vice-President.

**1671**

E. S. CARL., Cashier.
F. C. KROEGER, Ass't Cashier.

# Citizens National Bank,

## DAVENPORT, IOWA.

### UNITED STATES DEPOSITORY.

**COMPTROLLER'S CALL, SEPT. 20, 1898.**

| Resources. | | Liabilities. | |
|---|---|---|---|
| Loans and Discounts, . . . | $697,758.42 | Capital Stock, . . . . . | $300,000.00 |
| U. S. Bonds, . . . . . | 180,038.32 | Surplus Fund, . . . . . | 100,000.00 |
| Other Bonds, . . . . . | 50,000.00 | Undivided Profits, . . . . | 9,920.63 |
| Furniture and Fixtures, . . | 5,000.00 | Circulation, . . . . . | 90,000.00 |
| Due from Banks, . . . . | 510,734.21 | Deposits, . . . . . . | 1,035,154.18 |
| Cash and U. S. Treas., . . | 91,543.86 | | |
| Total, . . . . | $1,535,074.81 | Total, . . . | $1,535,074.81 |

### DIRECTORS.

T. W. McCLELLAND.
ROBERT KRAUSE.
W. C. WADSWORTH.
J. J. RICHARDSON.

H. O. SEIFFERT.
P. T. KOCH.
A. W. VANDERVEER.

OTTO ALBRECHT.
F. H. GRIGGS.
J. LORENZEN.
H. H. ANDRESEN.

---

H. H. ANDRESEN, President.
H. LISCHER, Vice-President.

CHAS. N. VOSS, Cashier.
J. F. BREDOW, Ass't Cashier.

## Cash Capital, - - - - $500,000.00

# German Savings Bank,

## DAVENPORT, IOWA.

### Statement of September 30, 1898.

**ASSETS.**

| | | | | | |
|---|---|---|---|---|---|
| Loans secured by Mortgages, | . | . | . | $3,366,319.68 | |
| Loans secured by Collaterals, Bonds, etc., | | . | . | 1,244,199.39 | |
| Total Loans, | . | . | . | | $4,610,519.07 |
| Cash on Hand and in Banks, | . | . | . | $543,412.23 | |
| Cash in Transit, | . | . | . | 73,193.25 | |
| Total Cash, | . | . | . | | $616,605.48 |
| Real Estate, | . | . | . | . | 80,125.68 |
| Total Assets, | | | . | . | $5,307,250.23 |

**LIABILITIES.**

| | | | | |
|---|---|---|---|---|
| Deposits, | . | . | . | $4,622,845.64 |
| Capital Stock, | . | . | . | 500,000.00 |
| Undivided Profits, | . | . | . | 184,404.59 |
| Total Liabilities, | . | . | | $5,307,250.23 |

### DIRECTORS.

OTTO ALBRECHT.  H. LISCHER.  H. O. SEIFFERT.  H. H. ANDRESEN.  JENS LORENZEN.
CHARLES N. VOSS.  F. H. GRIGGS.  T. A. MURPHY.  L. WAHLE.

iii

iv

GOVERNMENT BUILDING, DAVENPORT.

vi

—  -ORGANIZED 1871. - -

T. J. ROBINSON, President.  J. H. WILSON, Vice-President.  J. F. ROBINSON, Cashier.

**No. 1880**

# Rock Island National Bank,

## UNITED STATES DEPOSITORY,

### *ROCK ISLAND, ILL.*

*Capital,* . . . . . *$100,000.00*   *Surplus,* . . . . . *$75,000.00*

―――――――――*DIRECTORS*――――― - ―

| | | | |
|---|---|---|---|
| T. J. ROBINSON. | J. H. WILSON. | F. C. A. DENKMANN. | PETER FRIES. |
| E. D. SWEENEY. | CHAS. L. WALKER. | H. S. HANSON. | J. F. ROBINSON. |

NEW POST OFFICE, ROCK ISLAND.

viii

MOLINE POST OFFICE BUILDING.

x

TURNER HALL, DAVENPORT.

xii

# The Federal Life Association

## OF DAVENPORT, IOWA,

Has long since passed the experimental stage of its existence, and bases its claims for public patronage upon its unassailable record, its experience and the intrinsic merit of its plans.

### Organized under the stringent laws of Iowa,

It is submitted that this Company is especially deserving of consideration by those who seek for their families protection of the most absolute character at the lowest cost attainable by intelligent management, prudence and economy.

It has achieved a reputation second to none, and is worthy of every confidence reposed in it, and is eminently deserving of the prosperity it has enjoyed in the past and will continue to experience in the future.

COL. HENRY EGBERT, President.        E. H. WHITCOMB, Secretary and General Manager.

### DIRECTORS.

HENRY EGBERT, Egbert, Fidler & Chambers, Publishers.
ERASTUS BENSON, Attorney at Law.
E. B. HAYWARD, Wholesale Lumber.
S. D. BAWDEN, Cashier, Davenport National Bank.
A. V. MARTIN, American Luxfer Prism Co.
THOS. THOMPSON, Books, Stationery, etc.
E. H. WHITCOMB, Secretary, Federal Life Association.
DR. WM. D. MIDDLETON, Surgeon-in-Chief, C. R. I. & P. R'y.

YOUNG MEN'S CHRISTIAN ASSOCIATION BUILDING, ROCK ISLAND.

Rock Island, Ill.

# To the American People:

The **Modern Woodmen of America** is the leading Fraternal Beneficiary Society in the land. Its claim to preëminency is based upon its restricted territory, selected risks, low (35.76) average age, its exclusion of extra hazardous employments and its conservative business management.

Assessments for the discharge of mortuary liabilities are graduated according to the age of the applicant, which are not thereafter increased. The maximum limit is forty-five years; one past that age is ineligible to beneficiary membership.

Its form of government is representative and uninterruptedly within the control of its membership. Its legislative power is its Head Camp, composed of delegates elected and convening biennially. This body, fresh from the membership, enacts the Society's laws and defines its policy.

Its financial affairs are protected by an admirable system of checks and counter-checks, rendering fraud and deception practically impossible. No dollar can be disbursed from its funds without the signature of its Head Consul, Head Clerk and a majority of its Board of Directors.

It is a corporation, chartered by the State of Illinois May 5, 1884.

In no year has its membership been called upon to contribute more than eleven assessments and in the past two years ten have sufficed to discharge its mortuary liabilities in full.

In the fifteen years of its history $11,272,594.95 has been disbursed to the beneficiaries of its 5,535 deceased members.

The growth of the Society has been phenomenal, evidencing its popularity with its constituency — the people of the Great Northwest. Commencing with a modest bid for business in 1884, it had attained a membership of 42,694 in 1890. It now has 340,000 members, and 1,500,000 beneficiaries look to it for protection.

The headquarters of the Society are now in its new and elegant fireproof building at Rock Island. It is a neighbor to the greatest Arsenal in the world.

Very truly yours,

*Head Clerk, M. W. of A.*

xiv

THE NEW HOME OF THE MODERN WOODMEN OF AMERICA, ROCK ISLAND, ILL.

# The Kimball House

AMERICAN PLAN

---

✻ ✻ ✻ Rates: $2.00, $2.50, $3.00 per day ✻ ✻ ✻

---

## H. W. Sommers, Proprietor

(Formerly of the Virginia and Metropole Hotels of Chicago.)

BLACK HAWK INN.— Open from May to October 1.

xvi

xviii

DAVENPORT PUBLIC LIBRARY.

xix

xx

NEW COURTHOUSE, ROCK ISLAND.

xxi

xxii

A. Burdick, Prest.              H. H. Andresen, Vice-Prest.              F. G. Clausen, Sec'y and Treas.

E. B. DAWES, Sup't.

# Davenport Canning and Conserving Co.

## DAVENPORT, IOWA,

——————PACKERS OF——————

LITTLE DUKE PEAS.
EARLY CLUSTER JUNE PEAS.
DAVENPORT BRAND SUGAR CORN.
SEAL OF IOWA SUGAR CORN.
BASKET BRAND SUGAR CORN.

GOLDEN SLIPPER SUGAR CORN.
BATTLE AX BRAND SUGAR CORN.
WILD ROSE SUGAR CORN.
GOLDEN SHEAF SUGAR CORN.

# WASHBURN-HALLIGAN COFFEE CO.

MANUFACTURERS OF THE "PURE QUILL" BRANDS OF

# Baking Powder, Flavoring Extracts & Ground Spices

IMPORTERS AND JOBBERS OF HIGH-GRADE

## TEAS, COFFEES AND SPICES.

OUR LEADING BRANDS OF COFFEES ARE

O. G. JAVA and MOCHA,          P. Q. JAVA and MOCHA,
CUCUTA JAVA and MOCHA,          AMBER JAVA and MOCHA.

Our Coffees are selected from the best coffee-producing countries in the world, carefully blended, fresh roasted, absolutely pure. Order from your grocer.

*DAVENPORT, IOWA.*

MOLINE CLUB—INTERIOR VIEW.

xxiii

STATIONS:

MAIN OFFICE AND WORKS, OIL CITY, PA

CHICAGO, ILL.
BURLINGTON, IOWA.
NEW YORK, N. Y.

ROCK ISLAND, ILL.
PHILADELPHIA, PA.
HAMBURG, GERMANY.

AMSTERDAM AND ROTTERDAM, HOLLAND.

Schricker-Rodler Company
MARBLE GRANITE

STATUARY, MANTELS, GRATES AND TILING.

CORNER THIRD AND RIPLEY STS

DAVENPORT, IOWA.

FEJERVARY
HOME FOR AGED MEN, DAVENPORT.

xxv

xxvi

The best and cheapest light is gas with incandescent burners.

*Use gas stoves for cooking and heating*

# Davenport Gas and Electric Company.

BROADWAY PRESBYTERIAN CHURCH, ROCK ISLAND.

MOLINE HIGH SCHOOL.

**JOHN DEERE,**
PIONEER PLOW MANUFACTURER,
FOUNDER OF
DEERE & COMPANY.
1847.


xxx

# LIST OF ILLUSTRATIONS.

## THE ARSENAL, ISLAND AND CANAL.

# LIST OF ILLUSTRATIONS.

## THE ARSENAL, ISLAND AND CANAL — *Continued.*

FACSIMILE OF AUTHORITY FOR THE ILLUSTRATIONS IN THIS WORK.

---

**ROCK ISLAND ARSENAL**

ROCK ISLAND

May 6th 1898.

Dear Mr.Tillinghast:-

Under instructions from
the Chief of Ordnance,permission is hereby accorded you to take views of buildings,grounds,
or shops (exterior and interior) at this Arsenal.

Respectfully

Capt.Ord.Dept.U.S.A.

Commanding.

Mr.B.F.Tillinghast,

Davenport,Iowa.

---

*All the views not otherwise credited are reproductions of photographs specially taken for "Rock Island
Arsenal: in Peace and in War," by Mr. J. E. CALKINS, under the most favorable conditions.*

---

REAR VIEW OF THE NORTH ROW OF SHOPS.

# ROCK ISLAND ARSENAL:

## IN PEACE AND IN WAR.

WITH MAPS AND ILLUSTRATIONS.

(Extract from an official letter from Brigadier-General S. V. Benet, Chief of Ordnance, to Hon. George W. McCrary, Secretary of War, March 30, 1877.)

"THIS ARSENAL WILL BE THE GRAND ORDNANCE MANUFACTURING ESTAB-
LISHMENT IN THE MISSISSIPPI VALLEY, ERECTED AT GREAT EXPENSE
TO THE UNITED STATES, AND WITH A LARGER CAPACITY,
WHEN COMPLETED, THAN ANY OTHER ARSENAL
WITHIN OUR BORDERS."

By B. F. TILLINGHAST,

AUTHOR OF "THREE CITIES AND ROCK ISLAND ARSENAL."

"The Valley of the Mississippi is, upon the whole, the most magnificent dwelling-place prepared by God for man's abode."— *De Tocqueville's Democracy in America.*

CHICAGO:
THE HENRY O. SHEPARD COMPANY, PRINTERS.
1898.

TWENTY-THREE HUNDRED ARSENAL WORKMEN.

*From a photograph taken by Lieut. O. C. Horney, July, 1898.*

# THREE ARSENAL CITIES.

The center of population has moved westward (in ten years) about forty-eight miles and northward about nine miles. It now rests in southern Indiana, about twenty miles east of Columbus.

The center of the area of the United States, excluding Alaska (and the new possessions in the Pacific Ocean), is in northern Kansas, in approximate latitude 39° 55' and approximate longitude 98° 50'. — *Federal Census, 1890.*

[The movement of the center of population has been westward at the rate of five miles a year since 1790.]

T HE Upper Mississippi Valley — the most fertile section of equal area in the world — has its center of industrial activity in the three cities which overlook the Island of Rock Island. This Island is one of the largest, and by far the most beautiful, in the Father of Waters.

Together these cities have a population of some eighty thousand, about equally divided by the great river. This busy community may have a special local interest in the Island and in Rock Island Arsenal, but this vast plant has been built and is maintained by the people of the United States for national uses. Strictly speaking, the Arsenal is in no sense more local than the Capitol at Washington, a transcontinental line of railway or the long and deep artery of trade which floats an immense commerce from St. Paul to New Orleans.

It is not in the least material or significant in what order these closely linked cities — a trinity in unity — are named. Moline, Rock

PIER OF THE FIRST BRIDGE.

Island and Davenport, Rock Island, Davenport and Moline, and Davenport, Moline and Rock Island all convey the underlying fact of a common and inseparable interest. The Island is the park and the pride of each, and it is the unwritten law that no one city has an advantage over the other in this respect. There are many other interests which bind them together and promote the common good. Some of these may be mentioned.

5

## BRIDGES.

The Government owns and controls all bridges reaching the Island, and they are ample for any possible needs. A moss-covered stone pier, a third of a mile above the present main structure spanning the river, shows the location of the first

NO. 2. FIRST BRIDGE ACROSS THE MISSISSIPPI AS REBUILT AFTER DAMAGE BY FIRE, ICE AND COLLISION.

6

bridge across the Mississippi from its mouth to its source. It was built by the Chicago, Rock Island & Pacific Railway Company. It was a single-deck, Howe-truss, six-span bridge. The first train, consisting of locomotive and eight cars, passed over it April 21, 1856. On the 6th of May, that year, the first span east of the draw, 250 feet in length, was destroyed by fire, communicated by the steamboat Effie Afton, which collided with and burned at one of the piers. In March, 1868, with the opening of the river, the first pier from the Iowa shore was, by the heavy floating ice, pushed bodily downstream some twenty-five feet. The ensuing month, during a severe windstorm, the draw span was lifted from its masonry and blown

LOOKING TOWARD DAVENPORT FROM ISLAND CLOCK TOWER.

over on its side up-river, so that it hung supported only by the draw pier, with both ends free in midair.

The second bridge was completed in October, 1872, and turned over to the commanding officer of the Arsenal in February, 1873. It was built jointly by the Government and the railroad company. Its total length was 1,550 feet, divided into five spans and one draw. Its cost was not far from $1,000,000.

This structure served until the present bridge, constructed during the winter of 1894 and 1895, succeeded it on the old piers. It is a double-decked superstructure, with double railroad track above and double street-car track and wagon road below. The trusses of this thoroughly modern bridge are calculated to carry a total moving load of 11,360 pounds per lineal foot, of which 8,000 pounds are on the railway

floor and 3,360 pounds on the roadway floor. The solid corrugated steel railway floor, together with the guard angles and rail plates, weigh about 940 pounds per lineal foot of the bridge. The draw span, which weighs, approximately, 2,500,000

THE MOLINE BRIDGE.

pounds, is one of the heaviest ever built. The chain motion for moving this span is one of the departures from the usual methods of bridge building. Beginning at the north end, the first span is 260 feet long ; the second, third and fourth are each 220 feet long ; the fifth is 260 feet, and the total length of the draw is 368 feet. The open space on either side of the draw pier is 162 feet. The approach span on the Davenport side is 200 feet in length and on the Island end practically one-half this length. Ralph Modjeska, son of the noted actress, was chief engineer of the new bridge, and the Phœnix Bridge Company was the builder of both structures at the present site.

At the southwest limit of the Island there is a wagon bridge, the way being twenty-two feet in the clear, in the form of a viaduct under which trains pass. There are foot walks outside the chords, each six feet wide. At its eastern or upper end a bridge is also thrown across the south branch, known as Sylvan Water, connecting the Island with the city of Moline. The length of this bridge is 711 feet. It has five equal spans of 142 feet.

THE LION'S HEAD.
Gargoyle on Bridge over Island Lake.

9

## BRIDGE AND RIVER TRAFFIC.

The river is always unobstructed, except by ice, but the Government requires that a record be kept of the traffic through the draw, how many times it is opened, and the stage of the water every day in the year. Valuable information is thereby gathered. The following table tells much but by no means all of the business on and through the principal bridge. It takes no account, for instance, of the hundreds of thousands of street-car passengers. It does not give the freight tonnage. During 1897 the number of tons of freight hauled across the bridge by railroad was 2,069,602, as compared with 164,653 forty years earlier. This indicates the marvelous development that is going on.

Following is an epitome of the bridge traffic for the twelve months ended June 30, 1898 :

| | | |
|---|---|---|
| Engines with trains, north, | . . . | 9,083 |
| Engines with trains, south, | . . . | 9,582 |
| Engines, north, | . . . . . . | 1,206 |
| Engines, south, | . . . . . . | 896 |
| Passenger cars, north, | . . . | 17,048 |
| Passenger cars, south, | . . . | 16,949 |
| Freight cars, north, | . . . . . | 130,993 |
| Freight cars, south, | . . . . . | 132,514 |
| Street cars, north, | . . . . | 45,326 |
| Street cars, south, | . . . . . . | 45,568 |
| Teams, north, | . . . . . . | 256,494 |
| Teams, south, | . . . . . . | 254,839 |
| Pedestrians, north, | . . . . . | 336,324 |
| Pedestrians, south, | . . . . . | 335,143 |
| Steamboats, up river, | . . . . . | 1,656 |
| Steamboats, down river, | . . . | 1,653 |
| Barges, up river, | . . . . . . | 419 |
| Barges, down river, | . . . . | 413 |
| Rafts, down river, | . . . . . . | 474 |
| Strings of logs, down river, | . . . | 4,441 |
| Strings of lumber, down river, | . . | 639 |

A railroad and terminal bridge, not connected with the Island, but joining the three cities, is now nearing completion, at a cost of more than a million dollars, including the approaches.

## RIVER, RAPIDS AND CANAL.

The Mississippi River is the country's free waterway for nearly two thousand miles — exactly speaking, 1,982. At low water the river at Rock Island is 534 feet above sea-level. The section of river known as Rock Island Rapids extends from the lower end of the Island nearly fourteen miles up the river, the fall in this distance being twenty-one feet. From the head of the wing dam to the west end of the Island the distance is 3.20 miles. The fall of the rapids here is 6.65 feet at high water and 7.55 feet at low water. The improvement of the river channel through the rapids has engaged the Government's best engineering talent for many years. Surveys of Rock Island Rapids were made by Lieut. N. B. Buford in 1829, by H. M. Shreve in 1836, by Lieuts. Robert E. Lee and M. C. Meigs in 1837, Lieutenant Warren in 1853 and by others at later dates. Public attention has been repeatedly called to the great water-power advantages, now partially utilized.

Four miles south of the Island is the western terminus of the Illinois and Mississippi Canal, one of the most important internal improvements the country has ever undertaken. Its relation to the Government's Arsenal as an added means of transportation is recognized. The subject is deserving of the more detailed attention it receives elsewhere in this book.

OVERLOOKING THE ISLAND FROM MOLINE BLUFFS.

11

## RAILROADS.

Several trunk lines of railroads and their connections are always ready to distribute the fabrications of the Arsenal expeditiously to any seaport or city in the United States. The transportation facilities are unlimited. Some of the railroads centering at the Arsenal are : The Chicago, Rock Island & Pacific ; the Chicago, Milwaukee & St. Paul ; the Chicago, Burlington & Quincy ; the Burlington, Cedar Rapids & Northern ; the Rock Island & Peoria.

## STREET CARS AND TELEPHONES.

The Tri-City Railway Company furnishes constant communication between the three cities by its excellent and extensive system of electric lines. There are forty-two miles of track, seventy-five motor and fifty other cars. The roadbed, equip-

THE LOWER END OF ROCK ISLAND.

ment, power house, barns, etc., represent a cost of $2,100,000. The passenger capacity of the system is unknown, but the highest number thus far carried in one day is 65,000. From one end of the line to the other the distance is eight miles. Nearly all railway stations, boat landings, public parks, Black Hawk's tower and other places of interest are on or near the street-car lines.

Another means of communication between the two sides of the river is the Rock Island and Davenport Ferry.

One of the first telephone exchanges in the West was introduced here, and it is now one of the largest in proportion to population. The number of telephones in use is 1,450 in the three cities. There is no toll charged, the exchange, like the street-car system and the banks, doing an uninterrupted business, as if State and municipal boundaries did not exist.

# THE PRESS.

There are ten daily papers in the three cities, all working in accord for the general good. In fact, their editors, publishers and reporters have an organization which meets at regular intervals to consider and promote the interests of the community. These journals, in the order of their establishment in each city, are : The *Evening Democrat, Der Demokrat* (morning), *Evening Times, Evening Leader* and *Republican* (morning), in Davenport ; the *Evening Argus* and the *Union* (morning), Rock Island ; the *Evening Dispatch, Evening Republican-Journal* and *Evening Mail*, Moline. There are several semi-weekly, weekly and monthly publications.

FORT ARMSTRONG AVENUE.

## A FINANCIAL CENTER.

The three Arsenal cities together form a financial Gibraltar, with ample capital for all legitimate transactions. This is a statement of fact, not of mere opinion, and is warranted by the latest sworn statements of the several institutions. The eight national banks in the three cities make this showing :

| DAVENPORT. | CAPITAL. | SURPLUS AND PROFITS. |
|---|---|---|
| Citizens National, . . . . . . | $300,000 | $119,000 |
| First National, . . . . . | 200,000 | 70,000 |
| Davenport National, . . . . | 175,000 | 32,000 |
| Iowa National, . . . . . . | 100,000 | 18,000 |
| ROCK ISLAND. | | |
| Rock Island National, . | 100,000 | 82,303 |
| People's National, . . | 100,000 | 68,073 |
| MOLINE. | | |
| First National, . . . . | 150,000 | 37,892 |
| Moline National, . . . . | 100,000 | 23,521 |
| Total, . . | $1,225,000 | $450,789 |

To these totals should be added the capital and surplus of the private bank of Mitchell & Lynde, which does a business larger than the average of the eight national banks.

No business center of equal population in the entire Northwest is able to make so eloquent an exhibit in the way of its savings bank deposits, a certain index of the thrift of the people and of their industry.    These are as follows :

| DAVENPORT. | CAPITAL. | DEPOSITS. |
|---|---|---|
| German Savings, . . . . . . | $500,000 | $4,430,000 |
| Davenport Savings, . . . . . | 250,000 | 2,063,170 |
| Scott County Savings, . . . . | 250,000 | 2,023,000 |
| Union Savings, . . . . . . | 60,000 | 333,000 |
| Farmers and Mechanics Savings, . | 100,000 | 359,000 |
| ROCK ISLAND. | | |
| Rock Island Savings, . | 100,000 | 1,019,238 |
| MOLINE. | | |
| Moline Savings, . . . . . . | 100,000 | 523,000 |
| People's Savings, . . . . . . | 100,000 | 311,481 |
| Total, . . | $1,460,000 | $11,061,889 |

Here is a banking capital of $2,785,000 and surplus and profits amounting to $923,392 for the seventeen institutions — national, private and savings banks.    They hold individual deposits aggregating, at the time of their latest statements, $14,987,450.

THE ARSENAL MASCOT.

### THE ILLINOIS SIDE.

The boundary line separating Illinois from Iowa, midriver, places the Island in Illinois.    On that side are the industrial cities of Rock Island and Moline, covering more than five miles of water frontage.    The municipal limits of Moline on the east extend beyond the head of the Island, and those of the city of Rock Island far below or to the west and south.    The bluffs approach within half a mile of the river in Upper Moline and recede from it as they follow the Mississippi to the lower end of Rock Island.    The heights all the way are crowned with homes of comfort. Desirable residence sites are occupied below the bluffs, the fall being gradual to the bank.    The business sections and railroads are generally near the river.    In all that goes to make cities inviting — schools, churches, libraries, waterworks, public buildings, hospitals, good streets, well-to-do people, factories, jobbing houses, stores, parks — Rock Island and Moline are favored.    Their manufactures are known throughout the world.    The United States engineer's office has for years been located in Rock Island.    It has charge of the Mississippi River improvements from St. Paul to the mouth of the Illinois River.

### THE IOWA SIDE.

Opposite the eastern point of the Island, on the Iowa side, the rather sharp bluffs run out to the river.    Here begins a narrow plateau, which gradually widens as one looks toward the west for four miles, when it approaches the bend made by the river in turning south. The bluffs have a wavy or broken appearance, affording many choice views or lookouts. At the east, facing the Island, and almost opposite the immense shops, the city of Davenport has graded a projecting height and named it Prospect Park. Some three miles farther down is another small public park, from which a magnificent view, both up and down the valley, is obtained. Between the line of hills and the river the triangular-shaped plateau, gently sloping to the south, is ample for the accommodation of 150,000 people. The drainage is naturally good, street rising above street on the sides of the bluffs, like terraces. Back of the heights rich rolling prairie extends to the north, east and west.

MAIN ENTRANCE TO ARSENAL.

Davenport may pardonably boast of its educational institutions, both public and private, of its many charitable institutions, its schools and churches, its library, Academy of Natural Sciences, of its unsurpassed filtered-water system, its parks, wholesale and retail houses, cathedrals (being the See city of the Episcopal and Roman Catholic churches), factories of numerous kinds,— in brief, of its thrift and substantial progress.

But the purpose of "ROCK ISLAND ARSENAL: IN PEACE AND IN WAR" is told on its title-page. It does not pretend to more than glance at the environment of the Island. The three cities of themselves furnish subject-matter for a volume.

# THE ISLAND OF THE INDIANS.

This was the best Island on the Mississippi and had long been the resort of our young people during the summer. It was our garden (like the white people have near their big villages), which supplied us with strawberries, blackberries, plums, apples, and nuts of various kinds ; and its waters supplied us with pure fish, being situated in the rapids of the river. In my early life I spent many happy days on this Island. A good spirit had care of it, who lived in a cave in the rocks immediately under the place where the fort (Armstrong) now stands, and has often been seen by our people. He was white, with large wings like a swan's, but ten times larger. We were particular not to make much noise in that part of the Island which he inhabited, for fear of disturbing him. But the noise of the fort has since driven him away, and no doubt a bad spirit has taken his place.— *Black Hawk, through his interpreter, Antoine Le Claire.*

THE Island is a fascinating subject for the historian, but the past is so crowded by matters of present moment that little more than the order of events can be given for almost one hundred and fifty years.

BLACK HAWK,
Or Ma-ka-tai-me-she-kia-kiak.

According to Francis Parkman in his " Discovery of the Great West," Louis Joliet and Jacques Marquette first saw the Island in the summer of 1673.

Ninety-four years later Ma-ka-tai-me-she-kia-kiak, or Black Hawk, the Sac chief, was born on Rock River, a few miles south of the Island. He died in 1838, at the age of seventy-one years.

By the treaty with Great Britain in 1783 the United States was placed in possession of the east bank of the Mississippi River.

The United States gained its right to the Island of Rock Island through the Harrison treaty with the chiefs of the Sac and Fox tribes of Indians, made at St. Louis in November, 1804.

The Island was not definitely occupied by white men, and appears to have had no history, until the breaking out of the war with Great Britain in 1812. The first incident of that war which came home to the Island was Governor Clark's expedition to Prairie du Chien. It was attacked by the Indians and nearly destroyed. Campbell's Island, five miles above, was the scene of a conflict in which thirty-six soldiers were killed.

December 24, 1814, the treaty of Ghent was con-
cluded. September 13 and 14, 1815, treaties of peace
were made with the Sacs and Foxes.

It was in the year and month last named that Col.
R. C. Nichols, commanding the 8th United States Infantry, was sent up the Mississippi from St. Louis to estab-
lish a fort at or near Rock Island. The objects were to occupy the country, protect
coming settlers, control the Sacs and Foxes and guard travel and trade by river.

At that time the army was supplied with provisions by contractors directly, and
not through a commissary department as has since been the rule. George Davenport, after whom the city of Davenport was named, accompanied the expedition as
contractor's agent, and transported his supplies in light keel-boats. The expedition
reached the mouth of the Des Moines River, about 140 miles below the Island, and

BLACK HAWK DRIVE.

wintered there on account of the ice. In the following April, 1816, Gen. Thomas A. Smith arrived
at the cantonment with his rifle regiment, took
command, and proceeded up the river. He arrived
at the Island early in May, and fixed upon the foot
or west end as the site of a fort which was to be
built. The troops were first landed on the Island
May 10, 1816. They went into camp at once and
began cutting timber for storehouses. At that time
the west end of the Island, which is now bare,
except for trees that have been set out along the
drives, was covered with a heavy growth of oak,
black walnut, elm and basswood. General Smith
remained at the Island only long enough to construct abatis for the protection of the troops from
the Indians and then proceeded north with his rifle
regiment.

The 8th Infantry, under command of Colonel Lawrence, was left on the Island,
and under his direction the construction of Fort Armstrong was begun, the name
being chosen in honor of the secretary of war.

FIRING LYING.

17

FORT ARMSTRONG.

Completed 1817.   Evacuated May 4, 1836.

*Drawn from old sketches and historical descriptions for "Rock Island Arsenal; in Peace and in War," by Mrs. Alice C. Walker.*

# FORT ARMSTRONG.

Defenses, musters, preparations,
Should be maintain'd, assembled and collected
As were a war in expectation.—*Shakespeare.*

SEVERAL pictorial representations of this blockhouse defense called Fort Armstrong, of more than eighty years ago, exist. While no doubt they are generally correct, they differ materially in details. Gen. D. W. Flagler, Chief of Ordnance, in his valuable and unapproached "History of The Rock Island Arsenal," with every opportunity for investigation, says :

The interior of the fort was 400 feet square. The lower half of the walls was of stone, and the upper half of hewn timber. The timber and stone were procured on the Island. At three of the angles, the northeast, southeast and the southwest, blockhouses were built, and these were provided with cannon. One side of the square was occupied by the barracks and other buildings. These were built of hewn timber, with roofs sloping inward, as a protection against their being fired by the Indians, and that they might not furnish a safe lodging place for the enemy in an attack. The fort was placed on the extreme northwest angle of the Island. Its northwest corner was about 200 feet from the present location of the Island end of the bridge.

THE SUN DIAL.

Gov. Thomas Ford in his "History of Illinois" gives this description of Fort Armstrong as he saw it when approaching from the south (or west as the river runs) in the summer of 1831:

Fort Armstrong was built upon a rocky cliff on the lower point of an island near the center of the river, a little way above; the shores on each side, formed of gentle slopes of prairie extending back to bluffs of considerable height, made it one of the most picturesque scenes in the Western country. The river here is a beautiful sheet of clear, swift-running water, about three-quarters of a mile wide; its banks on both sides were uninhabited, except by Indians, from the lower rapids to the fort, and the voyager upstream after several days of solitary progress through a wilderness country on its borders came suddenly in sight of the whitewashed walls and towers of the fort, perched upon a rock surrounded by the grandeur and beauty of nature, which at a distance gave it the appearance of one of those enchanted castles in an uninhabited desert, so well described in the "Arabian Nights Entertainments."

As the fort neared completion the Indians showed a disposition to be more friendly, though the soldiers, numbering about six hundred, were watchful of attacks. "We did not object to their building the fort on the Island," Black Hawk is recorded as saying, "but we were very sorry."

In reference to the charmed cave in the rocks under the fort, the home of spirits, as Black Hawk imagined, General Flagler writes :

The cave was in the face of the limestone bluff at the northwest corner of the Island. At high water the floor of the cave was covered and boats could enter. This cave was closed, by building the abutment of the bridge across its entrance, in 1870.

Fort Armstrong was finished in 1817, but there were no exciting events until the outbreak of the Black Hawk War in 1831. Two companies of infantry were stationed there regularly. It was in reality a frontier post, visited by boats only at infrequent intervals. Judge Spencer, one of the first settlers on the Illinois side, relates that in 1828 mail was obtained by sending soldiers on foot to Galena, about one hundred miles north. In this way the news of General Jackson's election as President was brought to Rock Island garrison.

A stirring chapter of Western history is that which deals with the Black Hawk War—the last armed stand taken by the Indians to hold their lands east of the Mississippi. This is not properly within the writer's present scope. It may be said, however, that General Gaines, then at St. Louis, came to Fort Armstrong at the head of the 6th United States Infantry. The settlers were all moved to Rock Island, and General Gaines sent for the stubborn chief. Keokuk, too, with some of his warriors, attended the conference. War could not be averted, and in the hostilities that followed Lieut.-Col. Zachary Taylor (afterward President), Lieut. Jefferson Davis, Abraham Lincoln, and others who became of more than national prominence, took part. More than once the garrison on the Island was in imminent danger of massacre. The war continued until August 2, 1831, when, after several reverses, Black Hawk's band was practically destroyed. The old chief, his son Seoskuk and other chiefs were made prisoners and

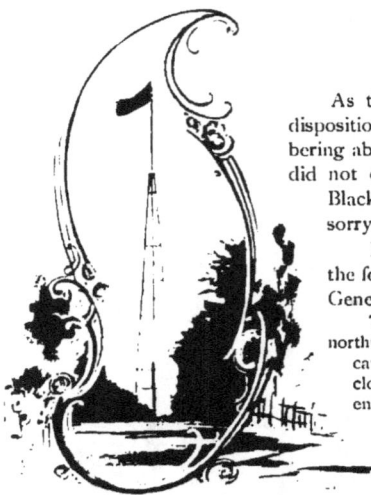

WHERE OLD GLORY ALWAYS WAVES.

GEN. WINFIELD SCOTT'S HEADQUARTERS, 1832.

brought to the Island, from which they were later taken to Washington. The Government took great pains to secure for Black Hawk a kind reception by the Indians upon his return from the East. The accounts of a meeting between the vanquished chief, Keokuk and others on the Island are very affecting. Black Hawk afterward established himself, with a remnant of his tribe, on the Des Moines River in Iowa, where he died in 1838.

Among the noted men who came to Fort Armstrong was Gen. Winfield Scott, and the occasion of his visit is deserving of notice. The hero of the Mexican War of sixteen years later was then forty-six. He was sent from the East with troops to direct the campaign against the Indians. He journeyed by way of the great lakes, Prairie du Chien and down the Mississippi, reaching Fort Armstrong in August, 1832. A virulent type of Asiatic cholera had broken out among the troops while on transports on the lakes, and it was brought with them to the Island. The cholera raged in its worst form in the large camp of jaded troops collected on the Island after the campaign, and was only broken up by distributing the troops in small camps on the bluffs along the west bank of the river. Several medical officers died, and General Scott, in a letter written not long after, ascribed the saving of the army from the scourge to the efforts of his chief medical officer, Surgeon C. A. Finley, afterward Surgeon-General during the Civil War.

NEAR THE CANNON'S MOUTH.

# THE ISLAND FROM 1832 TO 1862.

There's but the twinkling of a star
Between a man of peace and war.—*Butler in Hudibras.*

AT the close of the Black Hawk War Fort Armstrong had well served its object—a frontier defense. An end had come to Indian outbreaks and depredations, and the pioneers were free to claim the attractive country. The garrison was, however, maintained till May 4, 1836, when the fort was evacuated and the troops sent to Fort Snelling. Lieut.-Col. William Davenport, of the 1st Infantry, was in command at the time of the evacuation, and he left Lieut. John Beach in charge, with a few men, to take care of the property. But Fort Armstrong was never regarrisoned, and in November, 1836, the property that had been left was taken away.

GEORGE DAVENPORT.
The First White Settler on the Island,
May, 1816.
*From " Davenport Past and Present," by Franc B. Wilkie.*

General Street, Indian agent, had charge of the Island until 1838, when Col. George Davenport was appointed agent, and remained in charge till 1840. Colonel Davenport was the first white settler in the vicinity of the Island, his home for so many years. He was identified with it from 1815 to July 4, 1845, when he was murdered in his own home by an organized band of robbers and horse thieves. The murderers escaped unrecognized, but were afterward arrested, and three of them—Aaron Long, John Long and Granville Young—were executed on the 19th of the succeeding October.

Colonel Davenport was an Englishman, born in Lincolnshire in 1783. After many hard experiences at sea he reached New Orleans in 1806. During his Island years he became famous as a trader, winning the confidence of the Indians. His house, on the northern bank of the Island, now falling into decay, is shown in the illustrations.

22

In 1840 some of the buildings at Fort Armstrong were repaired, and an ordnance depot was established at the fort. Capt. W. R. Shoemaker was placed in charge of the depot and of the Island, and remained until 1845, when the stores were moved to St. Louis Arsenal.

From the year last named until the act for establishing Rock Island Arsenal was passed, in 1862, the Island was in charge of a civil agent, or custodian, employed by the War Department, and it has remained under the control of that department to this time.

Thomas L. Drum was custodian from 1845 to 1853; J. B. Danforth, from 1854 to 1857; H. Y. Slaymaker, from 1857 to 1863. The history of these eighteen years "is full of persistent and protracted efforts on the part of squatters, manufacturing, railroad, water-power companies and others to procure, by preëmption, lease, purchase or cession, a title to the lands on the Island." So it appears that the Island has been as great a prize in the eyes of the bargain-driving business men of recent times as it was in the consideration of Black Hawk and his band, who regarded it as their dearest possession.

COL. GEORGE DAVENPORT'S HOUSE.
1. As it was in 1860.      2. As it is in 1898.

1. A STATELY ELM.
2. A NATURAL GRAPE ARBOR.
3. WOODS EAST OF SHOPS.
4. IN THE JUNGLE.
5. THE LINDEN TREE.

# ADVANTAGES OF LOCATION.

After a careful study of this question of location, there is no position which, to my mind, affords so many advantages, and, at the same time, presents so few objections, as Rock Island, in the Mississippi River.

In a military point of view it is perfectly secure from an enemy advancing either by the lakes or the river. From it supplies can be transported in any direction and at any season of the year. It is in the midst of a country teeming with coal and wood, and especially adapted to agriculture. The site is elevated far above river floods, the climate and situation are healthy; and while the Island is sufficiently isolated to secure it from sudden attacks, it is near enough to the cities of Rock Island, Davenport and Moline to afford ample accommodations for all the necessary employes.— *General Ramsay, Chief of Ordnance, in a letter to the Secretary of War, 1864.*

THE chain of circumstances and events leading up to the great Arsenal of today is of continuous interest. Link has been added to link as administration has been succeeded by administration, until the rather rough plans of more than eighty years ago have developed into a system that is approaching perfection. Further on it will be seen that when a crisis came to the country in the spring of 1898, Rock Island Arsenal was prepared to meet the sudden and enormous demands made upon it for war material in a way that helped essentially in solving the difficulties of the Government. The day that peace was declared, after 114 days of hostilities, Senator Allison, of Iowa, who had supported every appropriation bill from the first, remarked that during the comparatively short war the Arsenal had more than repaid the country for the millions it had cost in the extent, variety and character of the equipments, stores and munitions it had so promptly furnished.

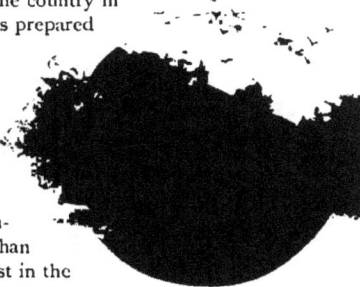

THE RESERVOIR.

It was on the 2d of March, 1825, that the Secretary of War informed the Commissioner of the General Land Office that the Island of Rock Island was necessary for military purposes, and directed that it be reserved from sale.

About the year 1835, by direction of Congress, two examinations of various sites for a Western armory were made by commissions of army officers. In September, 1840, the Chief of Ordnance, Colonel Talcott, directed the commanding officer at

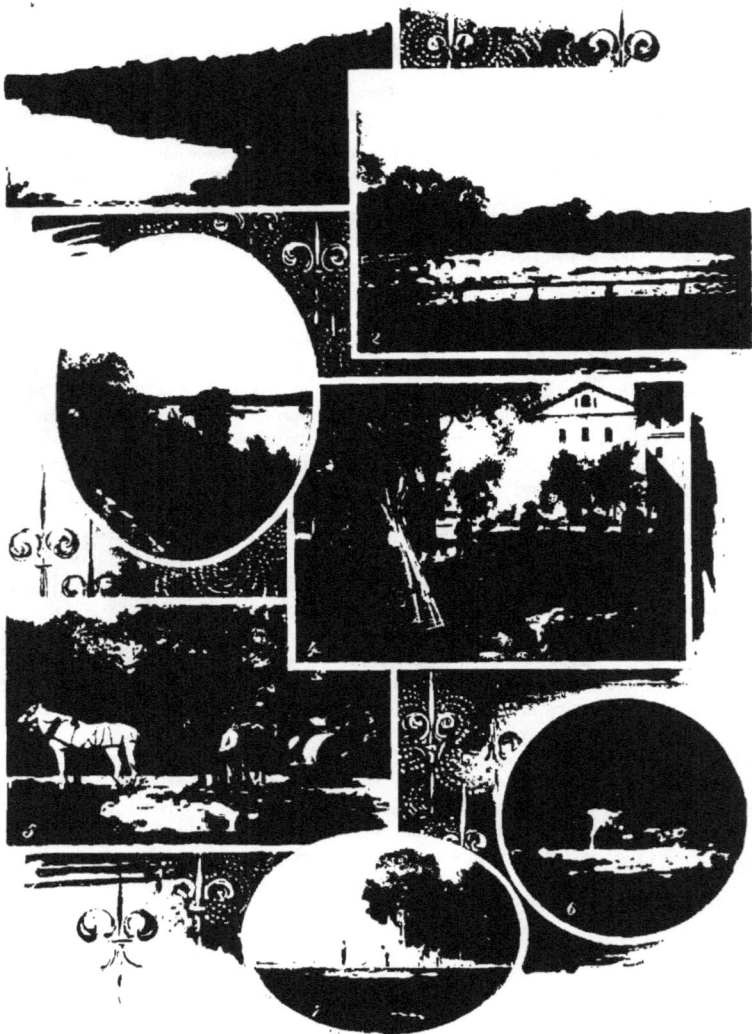

1. ALONG THE NORTH SHORE OF THE ISLAND.
2. AN ISLAND FARM.
3. THE DYKE AND PAPOOSE ISLAND.
4. SOLDIERS AS HAYMAKERS.
5. THE ROAD ROLLER.
6. NO THOUGHT OF WAR.
7. CLEANING UP.

St. Louis Arsenal to examine the Island of Rock Island with a view to its use for ordnance purposes. The resulting report made by Capt. William Bell shows the foresight and breadth of view of that officer. This is evidenced by the following extracts:

The whole Island, containing about 850 acres, belongs to the United States, having been specially reserved from sale. It lies at all times high and dry in the Mississippi, on the side of the Illinois shore, from which it is separated by about 600 or 700 feet; its greatest length, lying east and west, being about 2.61 miles, and its greatest breadth, lying north and south, being 1,463 yards; its perimeter, or circumference, being 6¼ miles.

There are but two occupants on the Island: one at the upper or east end, who has no claim upon the grounds; the other, at the north side, near the water, at the point marked "Davenport" on the accompanying sketch, which is the name of a very respectable gentleman who has lived there for many years, and who has gone to considerable expense in ornamenting the quarter section he claims, and in the erection of buildings thereon.

A PAPER TARGET.

Captain Bell's report accurately describes the Fort Armstrong buildings; recommends repairs; speaks in high terms of the towns (Rock Island, then Stevenson, and Davenport) on either side of the river; notes the good boat landings on the Island, and dwells at length on the great available water power afforded by the fall in the river. He was evidently captivated by the natural charms of the locality, for he writes that "the productiveness, health and beauty of the country surpass anything" he had seen.

In September, 1841, Congress passed an act for a thorough examination of the whole Western country "for the purpose of selecting a suitable site on the Western waters for the establishment of a national armory." The board of three officers spent eighteen months in making most thorough examinations, its report covering 400 printed pages. Much space was devoted to the Island and many exact facts were given. Some of the more salient features of the report are these:

This beautiful and interesting Island derives its name from the circumstances of its resting upon a bed of rocks, consisting of limestone in horizontal strata, well adapted to the purposes of building. It stands in the Mississippi, at the foot of Rock Island Rapids. Its length is about 2⅞ miles, and its greatest breadth four-fifths of a mile. It contains about 800 acres of excellent land, still the property of the United States. The surface of the Island is generally waving, and is pervaded by a broad valley passing centrally and longitudinally two-thirds the length of the Island. With the exception of a few acres cleared at the head of the Island (the site formerly occupied by Fort Armstrong, now used, in part, by the United States as a depot of arms for the Western country, and a large garden, with other improvements, occupied by George Davenport), the Island is covered with a dense timber growth. The Island is bounded, for the most part, by precipitous cliffs, or abrupt and rocky hill-stopes, its surface rising ten to twenty feet above the reach of the highest freshets.

This report, like the preceding one of Captain Bell, may, with entire moderation, be called enthusiastic in praise of the natural advantages offered by the Island for arsenal uses. The board of officers emphasizes the water-power opportunities, discusses the question of dams, the rapid fall in the river, the rich surrounding country, the nearness of beds of coal, lead and iron. "Articles of subsistence of all kinds," the commissioners say, "for man and beast, are abundant, and these are remarkably cheap. The site is exceptionally healthy, as evidenced by the reports, now on file in the office of the Surgeon-General, * * covering a period of more than twenty years, during which the number upon the sick list at Fort Armstrong was proportionately less than at any other post in the Western country."

Quartermaster-General Jesup, writing to the Secretary of War in 1852, says :

The site of Fort Armstrong, Rock Island, is one of the most valuable in our Western country for an armory. The whole water power of the Mississippi River is available. If a Western armory is to be established, I would advise that it be placed there. I would not advise that any part of it be rented or leased.

Hon. A. C. Dodge, Chairman Senate Committee on Public Lands, writing to the Secretary of War in 1854, says:

Rock Island, as you are well aware, has long been regarded by a large portion of the people of the Mississippi Valley as an advantageous site for an arsenal of construction.

Jefferson Davis, while Secretary of War, in 1854, was the stanch friend of Rock Island as the unequaled location for the Nation's mid-continent Arsenal, and likewise he was the advocate of river improvement. He had, twenty-two years earlier, from personal visitation, formed views which were never changed. Justice requires that credit be given Mr. Davis for using the authority of his position to prevent the sale of the Island to settlers, certain influences having been set in motion to secure that end while he held the portfolio of war.

Gen. C. P. Buckingham, October 24, 1862, wrote to the Secretary of War, after some time spent in a study of the Island :

MAIN AVENUE, NEAR MOLINE.

The Island is, without doubt, the best place for an Arsenal. It is high and healthy, well supplied with water from the Mississippi River, and the Chicago, Rock Island & Pacific Railroad is easily accessible. The Island contains about 900 acres of land, of which about 200 have been granted by Congress to individuals. The only question connected with the location of an Arsenal at this point is, I conceive, whether it shall be at the upper or lower end of the Island.

Without going further into the irrefutable arguments, it may be said that the full force of all these early observations has been far more than confirmed. The half century that has passed, the growth in population of the Upper Mississippi Valley and the vast region beyond, the coming of railroads and telegraphs, new discoveries of minerals, the partial utilization of water powers, the extensive river improvements, all these accentuate the reasons given so long ago for the location of the Government's largest Arsenal here.

Mere mention is all that can be made of the attempts to locate on the Island on the part of individuals and companies, of their temporary success, and of their ultimate exclusion through the purchase of their holdings obtained through franchises, the preëmption law, and other devious and questionable means. In one instance, where a settler had developed water power at the eastern end of the Island, he was paid $145,175 to relinquish his alleged or real rights.

PLANTED CANNON.

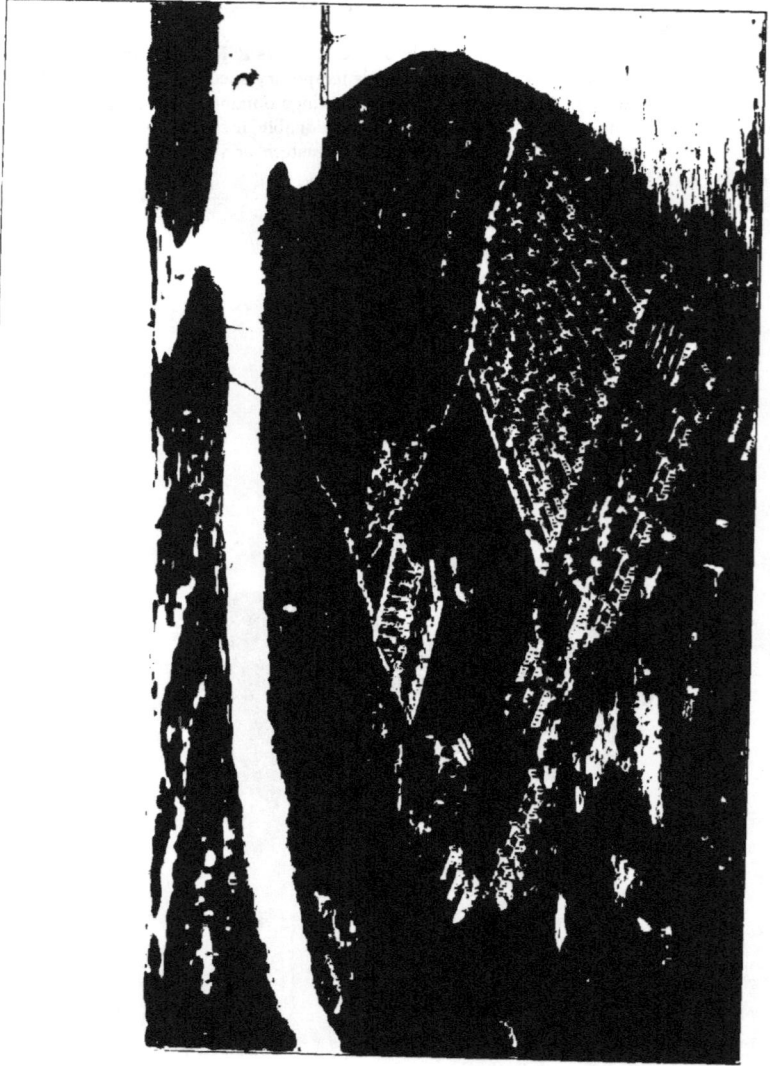

Pesthouse.      Officers' Quarters.      ROCK ISLAND MILITARY PRISON.      Hospital.      Prison Barracks.      First Mississippi River Bridge.

# THE ISLAND AS A MILITARY PRISON.

I am forbid
To tell the secrets of my prison-house.—*Shakespeare.*

D URING the war between the States, 1861-65, the Island was used for a purpose never intended by those who designed it for an Arsenal. It became
one of the largest military prisons in the North, through force of dire circumstances.
In the early stages of the Civil War, prisoners were captured both by the Union
forces and by the Confederates. These prisoners were
removed as far as possible from the scenes of hostilities.
Rock Island was owned by the Government; it was
hardly occupied; it was secure; it offered advantages
for the use to which it was put.

So extensive barracks for prisoners of war were
built in the summer and fall of 1863. The construction
of the buildings was in charge of Capt. C. A. Reynolds,
United States Quartermaster's Department, and they
were thought to be ample for the accommodation of
13,000 prisoners, though so large a number was never
quartered there at one time, or, as the records show,
altogether.

A full-page illustration shows with detail and accu-
racy not only the barracks, but all the buildings on the
Island at that time. The quarters for prisoners were
located on the north side, near the river front, a little
more than a mile from the lower or western end of the Island. The prison itself
took the form of a rectangle, covering about twelve acres. The four sides faced
nearly north, south, east and west. The northeast corner of the inclosure was opposite the lower point of Papoose Island. There were fourteen east-and-west rows oi
one-story frame buildings, six in a row. Each of the buildings or barracks was 100
feet in length by 20 in width, with windows on the sides and doors in the ends.
They were neither plastered inside nor painted outside, but well constructed for the
protection of the occupants. In one end — usually the west — of each building was
the kitchen. On either side of the long hall were rows of double-decked double

COL. A. J. JOHNSON, U. S. V.
Commandant Rock Island Military
Prison, 1864-65.

31

ROCK ISLAND MILITARY PRISON SCENES.

1. Bell Tower, Outside Entrance.
2. Prisoners Suffering Punishment Inflicted by Their Own Courts.
3. Administering the Oath of Allegiance.
4. View within the Stockade.
5. Prisoners Making Clam-Shell Trinkets.

berths or bunks for sleeping. Each building accommodated 120 persons. A main avenue, fifty feet wide, divided the seven rows on the north from the same number on the south.

Within these walls the prisoners were allowed as much liberty as possible. They were permitted to receive newspapers, magazines and books. Letters came to them every day from their Southern friends, though every piece of mail was opened and inspected and all remittances of money were taken out and receipts issued therefor, these receipts enabling the prisoners to buy such articles as were not

ROCK ISLAND MILITARY PRISON DAYS.
A. C. Dart.
Captain Bucher.        Maj. Frazer Wilson.      Capt. J. G. Robinson.

contraband. Packages of clothing and other goods were admitted after examination, and all privileges accorded Union soldiers confined in the South were extended to these Confederates. The name, home post office address, company and regiment of each prisoner was carefully recorded. They were in many cases permitted to work in clearing the Island grounds outside the prison. At one time more than forty carpenters, held as prisoners, were employed on other buildings it was found necessary to construct.

Extending around the prison barracks, some fifty feet from the sides and ends of the buildings, was the stockade. This was made of inch boards, twelve feet long,

ATTENTION, PLEASE!

placed on end. Four feet from the top was a platform or parapet wide enough to allow the sentinels to pass on their beats. Armed guards were always on duty. The "dead line," a sort of trench, paralleled the stockade about twenty-five feet distant on the inside. Two or three prisoners were shot while attempting to cross the "dead line." There were sentinel boxes or houses every hundred feet along the parapet. There were no successful plans of bodies of men to escape. The nearest approach to this was an underground tunnel on the south side of the prison. The tunnel was dug, but before an escape was effected the opening was discovered. Now and then a prisoner did get away, but it was next to impossible to leave the Island after scaling the stockade or getting through the gates.

The prisoners fared well, their rations being the same as those of the Union soldiers who performed guard and garrison duty. Some of them made money by their ingenuity and skill in converting clam shells into buttons and other devices. A number of them, after the war, were content to become residents of this locality. But it cannot be denied that disease entered the prison as it visited the camps of the Nation's soldiers in Tampa, Chickamauga, Fernandina and elsewhere during the war with Spain. The large buildings in the center of the Island, where the Arsenal shops now stand, show the Confederate hospital, and farther south, on the Illinois side, were the pesthouses. During the existence of the prison, 1,961 victims of disease died here and were buried on the Island.

Few traces of prison days remain. One wing of the old post hospital may be seen just east of the north row of shops, and west of the same row are two or three buildings used thirty-five years ago for officers' quarters. They were temporary structures, and nearly all of them have from time to time been removed. The illustration, however, is practically all that is left to recall this unpleasant feature of the Island's history.

The military prison was under the control of the commissary-general of prisoners, Brig.-Gen. William Hoffman, and was commanded during the first year after its construction by Col. Richard H. Rush, and after that by Col. A. J. Johnson, United States Volunteers. Doctor Watson, of Dubuque, was the surgeon in charge, and he was assisted in his duties by Dr. P. Gregg, of Rock Island, and many other physicians. A. C. Dart, now a wholesale merchant in Rock Island, was post sutler during the life of the prison, and probably has

PRESS FOR PRINTING TARGETS.

34

more records of the period than any other one individual. Thomas Winkless, ex-auditor of Scott County, Iowa, was chief clerk and bookkeeper in the office of the commissary of prisoners. Hornby & McClelland were the contractors who constructed the prison buildings, and the firm of French & Davies furnished the lumber. The cost of the barracks, hospitals, guardhouses, officers' quarters, etc., is estimated to have been more than $125,000. John Wilson Guiteau, now of New York City, was superintendent of construction under Quartermaster C. Q. A. Reynolds.

From the close of the Civil War to this time the national authorities have regarded the records of all the prisons as a sealed book, but the seal is to be broken. This is shown by the following letter from the chief of the Record and Pension Office of the War Department, under date of May 31, 1898, to the author of " Rock Island Arsenal : in Peace and in War " :

The United States military prison on Rock Island, Illinois, was opened about November 11, 1863, and closed about July 22, 1865. During that period there were 12,286 Confederate prisoners confined therein.

There are no published records of Rock Island military prison, but the records of the several prisons in use during the late war are in process of compilation and will soon be published in the series of Records of the War of the Rebellion.

This, from the Rock Island *Argus* of June 22, 1865, about the time the prison was closed, fittingly ends this chapter :

### THE ISLAND BURYING GROUNDS.

Above the hospitals, on the center road coming from Moline, out of sight from the Government buildings, secluded among the trees, lie the Confederate and Federal dead of Rock Island barracks.

> The reconciling grave
> Swallows distinctions first that make us foes,
> That all alike lie down in peace together.

Two neat yards, separate and secure, contain the remains of those who have died at the Island since the opening of the barracks. The first is the Federal burying ground, where repose the remains of some 200 Union soldiers, each grave having a headboard giving the name of the deceased, his company, regiment and date of death. A little distance beyond this graveyard, and also inclosed with a secure fence, is the Confederate burying ground, where about 2,000 Confederate prisoners of war lie buried. Their graves are in long, deep trenches, the bodies being placed separately in strong wooden boxes and laid side by side, about two feet apart. At the head of each is a board on which is painted the number of the grave and the initials of the deceased. On the books of the post, against each number, is found a complete description of the deceased, his company, regiment and State. Each of these graveyards is wholly cleared of trees, stumps, roots, stones, and the ground neatly sodded over.

BOYS COVERING CANTEENS.

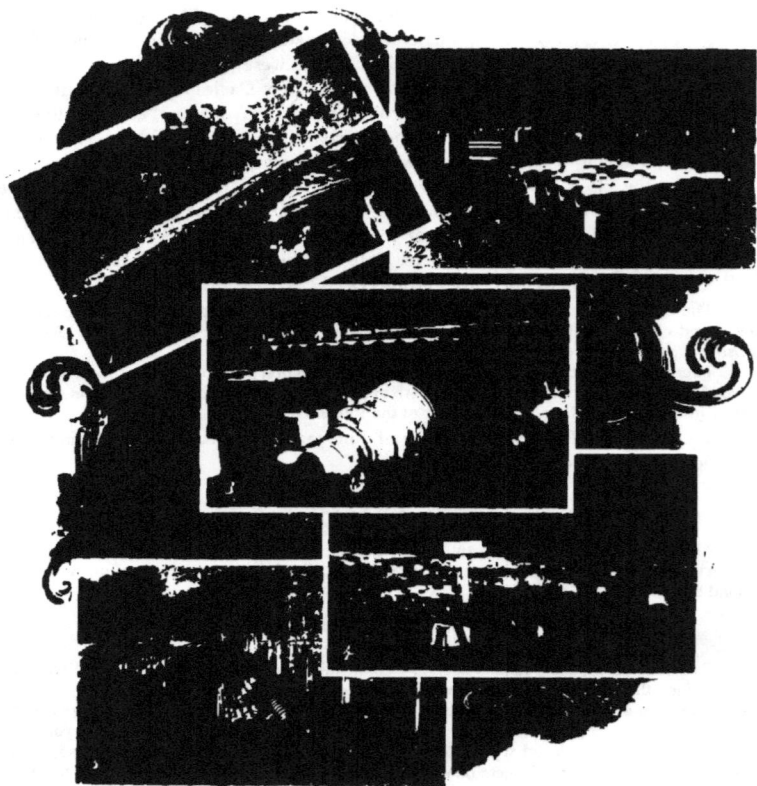

THE ARSENAL GUN YARD.

1. A View from Main Avenue.    4. Confederate Trophies.
2. The Seven Sisters.          5. Iron Posts, Chains and Cannon Balls.
3. A Trophy.

# FEATURES OF THE ISLAND.

*This beautiful and interesting Island.—Report of Board of Army Officers.*

## AREA AND CHARACTERISTICS.

TWO partial descriptions of the Island have been given : one by Captain Bell, written in 1840, the other by an army board one or two years later, but both underestimate the area and omit facts now better known.

The Island is not only the most beautiful, but it is one of the largest throughout the length of the Mississippi River. It is exceptional in the respect that a considerable part of it is above flood mark, and this advantage was particularly taken into account in fixing the site of the Arsenal buildings. From Chicago, the distance by rail is 181 miles; from the Missouri River at Council Bluffs, 316 miles. By river it is 332 miles north of St. Louis and 397 miles south of St. Paul. The Island is about two and three-fourths miles long, and varies in width from one-fourth to three-fourths of a mile. It contains, above low-water mark, 9 7 0 a c r e s. Lengthwise the Island lies nearly east and west, and the course of the Mississippi by the Island is generally about eleven degrees south of west. The highest ground on the Island is the part where the great shops are located, and this rises from 17 to 23 feet above the highest high water; the rest of the high ground is generally from 14 to 20 feet

1.   ISLAND GOLF LINKS.          2.   GROUP OF GOLFERS.

above a high stage of the river. All of the high ground rests on a foundation of gray magnesian limestone, which in places crops out on the surface, but it is mainly covered with from one to eight feet of earth, principally loam and clay, and sometimes sand, gravel and other earths.

## VARIETIES OF TREES.

The surface of the Island is waving, yet not to any marked extent, and it is covered generally, except the building sites, the avenues, the cemeteries and clearings for special purposes, with sparse timber. On much of it the first growth has been

37

THE ISLAND LAKE.

1. An Enchanted Spot.          3. Shadows in the Water.
2. The Bridge from Below.      4. Another View.

removed, and replaced by a second growth. For the most part the Government's grounds are kept trim and clean, and they have been beautified along the drives by setting out shade trees; but on the lower half of the south side of the Island nature has been almost undisturbed. Here the undergrowth is thick, and some of the trees indicate "the forest primeval." This adds to the attractiveness. The native trees are principally oak, elm, ash, basswood, hickory and walnut.

## AVENUES AND DRIVES.

The avenues east and west—that is to say, from Davenport and Rock Island to Moline—are graded, rolled and drained. They are always in perfect condition for driving. The two cross-avenues—north and south—are likewise smooth. A carriage road follows the river bank from the commandant's residence nearly to the head of the Island, where it crosses to the Moline bridge and then down the shore of Sylvan Water almost to the end. This drive shows the miles of dike or embankment that has been built to protect the lower parts of the Island from overflow. There are many drives, arched with interlocking branches, in all parts of the Island, which lead one to quiet retreats. Here the quail may be seen and the music of his whistle often heard. Feathered songsters find their home in large number, and all the year round the gray squirrels hold carnival.

## A PARADISE FOR BIRDS.

Shooting and trapping are not allowed on the Island, and dogs are not seen there. It may be said that from General Rodman's time to the present all the commandants have taken pains to preserve and protect the birds. The result is that their number has been increased and many varieties that are strangers to the surrounding country are to be seen. More than eighty varieties have been counted by bird-lovers, nearly all of them song birds. Of game birds, the visitor may see Quail, Pheasant, Snipe, Woodcock, Plover and Rail ; the Sap Sucker, Red-headed, Yellow-hammer and other Woodpeckers; Night, Hen and Sparrow Hawks; Rock, River and Mud Swallows ; also the Chippy, Sparrow, Red-Eyed Flycatcher, Bee Bird, Humming Bird, House Wren, Linnet, Indigo Bird, Bittern, Phebe, Red-bird, Snowbird, Bluebird, Kingfisher, Sand Martin, House Martin, Orchard Oriole, Blue Jay, Rose-breasted Grosbeak, Scarlet Tanager, Brown Thrush, Wood Thrush, Screech Owl, Great Horned Owl, Catbird, Red-winged Blackbird, Whippoorwill, King-bird, Robin, Cuckoo, Turtle Dove, Yellow-birds, and others. Nearly all of these birds nest and raise their young on the Island. Dense woodlands are sparse in this part of the country, and the heartless warfare of the hunter has nearly exterminated the birds. It is fortunate that parts of the Island have been left in their original state, and that they are a natural conservatory.

1. THE RODMAN GUN.          2. THE RODMAN MONUMENT.

## THE NATIONAL CEMETERY.

At the upper end of the Island, a few rods from the Moline entrance, lie the remains of nearly five hundred Union soldiers, most of whom died while serving at this post. The grounds are scrupulously cared for, and on each recurring 30th of May, Memorial Day, the graves are strewn with wreaths and flowers. It is the honored custom for thousands of the people of Davenport, Rock Island and Moline to gather there and hold patriotic services.

MEMORIAL DAY ON THE ISLAND.
1. The National Cemetery.    2. Around the Speaker's Stand.
3. Grand Army Veterans in Procession.

## GENERAL FLAGLER'S HISTORY.

The one standard and exhaustive "History of Rock Island Arsenal" is that written by Gen. D. W. Flagler. The early history is elaborately recounted. It was published by the War Department in 1877, a work of nearly 500 large pages, with numerous maps and plates. The volume may be consulted at the public library in each of the three cities.

## ISLAND PRIVILEGES.

Visitors hardly need to be reminded that army posts are not public parks, and that strict regulations are framed for their government. While the bridges are free at all times, a permit must be obtained, except on special occasions, in order to pass the guards at the entrances unchallenged. Smoking, shooting, racing, fast driving and interfering with the workmen are positively forbidden on the Island. Picnics and refreshments are not allowed. Flowers, plants and shrubs must not be disturbed. But between sunrise and sunset, every day, there is no trouble for either residents or visitors to see the Island, and it is not difficult to obtain permits to the shops. The hotels have passes for their guests, the liverymen for their patrons. Bicycle permits are granted on application, but the Island is not a highway for driving between the cities.

### AN ANCIENT BURIAL MOUND.

The antiquarian will find much of interest on the Island, an inviting field of investigation. The deposit of shells in the earth along the banks of the Mississippi has always attracted attention. Beds of considerable extent are found at the head of the Island. The layers are usually in horizontal position and vary from 3 to 4 centimeters to 1 meter in thickness. A valuable paper was presented to the Davenport Academy of Natural Sciences, February 28, 1873, by A. S. Tiffany, from which this extract is taken :

On the Rock Island Arsenal grounds, near the western extremity, there has been an excavation about 300 feet long and 80 feet deep. At a depth of 3 feet from the top is a deposit of shells, mostly *Unios*, but including *Melanthe Sub-solida*, and two or more species of *Helix*. This shell bed, at this exposure, varies from 6 to 16 inches in thickness. Accurate levelings prove the deposit to be 18 feet above the highest watermark known since Fort Armstrong was established on the Island (1817).

FORT FLAGLER.

In the lower part of this shell bed were found the skull and bones belonging to one individual. The bones were quite fragile, and easily fell to pieces, but a large portion of the skull was secured. There are many fragments, bearing witness that the whole skeleton had been there. Associated with these human remains were found the point of an antler of a deer or elk, and what appears to be a fragment of the shin bone of a bison which had apparently been broken to extract the marrow.

The covering was evidently an aqueous deposit, the sedimentary lines being perfect and unbroken. Deposited with and above the shells are gravel and sand, the material becoming finer toward the top, the last foot being fine alluvium and vegetable mold.

The section has been visited by many members of the Academy, and by Prof. Alexander Winchell, while some of the bones were in place, and all agree that the covering of this prehistoric man was a sedimentary deposit. It is believed that further investigation will accumulate many evidences that man was contemporaneous with this ancient shell bed.

Prof. W. H. Pratt, in a paper read before the Academy of Sciences August 17, 1877, says :

At the head of the Island, where are found the most extensive accumulations in this region, we find, at several places along the edge of the bank, an additional deposit of shells heaped up above the general shell bed, which is itself very heavy at the same point. One of these heaps is still over two meters high above the regular continuous bed, its contents being similar in every respect.   These superficial deposits slope off or thin out inland rather rapidly, extending back but a short distance from the present edge of the bank, and the face of the bank is vertical here down a meter or two to the solid limestone rock, being broken down and washed away by the high waters of every season, thus always presenting a good vertical section of the strata.

 * * * In this connection we ought not to overlook a bed of shells formerly existing near the foot of Rock Island, at the bottom of which the "shell-bed skull" was found by Mr. Tiffany in the fall of 1871.

Experience and examination of shell-bed mounds have fully convinced me that this was an ancient burial mound.

A TROPHY.

# THE COUNTRY'S ARSENALS.

The problem of preparation for war in modern times is both extensive and complicated.

The creation of material for war, under modern conditions, requires a length of time which does not permit the postponement of it to the hour of impending hostilities.

It is not the most probable of dangers but the most formidable that must be selected as measuring the degree of military precaution to be embodied in the military precautions to be maintained.

Material, once wrought into shape for war, does not deteriorate from its utility to the nation because not used immediately. It can be stored and cared for at a relatively small expense, and, with proper oversight, will remain just as good and just as ready for use as at its first production.

CAPT. A. T. MAHAN, recognized the world over as a high authority, has written impressively on the necessity of "Preparedness for War," and the foregoing extracts leave no doubt about his meaning. The nations of the earth have accepted it as conclusive, and their armies and navies are larger and stronger than ever before. It has been the policy of the United States from the first. It has built and maintained arsenals and armories, an increasing navy, seacoast defenses, and the military and naval schools in which to give practical and efficient training in war. But it has done all this with a moderation that at times has not given the feeling of security that is the right of the people. To maintain its honor and integrity, and on grounds of broad humanity, our country has been forced into war when it was not ready. What if England, Germany, France or Russia had been our foe in the last war? No sane citizen can doubt that the cost of life and treasure would have been incalculably greater, the conflict of longer duration and the loss to some, at least, of the seacoast cities frightful to contemplate.

ELM DRIVE.

But the war with Spain, which has won such brilliant achievements for our arms, has only added new and weighty reasons—invincible arguments—for extending

43

HEAVY ORDNANCE.

1. Siege Howitzer, 7-inch.
2. Siege Gun, with Breech Open.
3. Siege Gun, 5-inch, Firing Position.
4. Siege Gun, Traveling Position.
5. Field Gun, 3.2-inch.

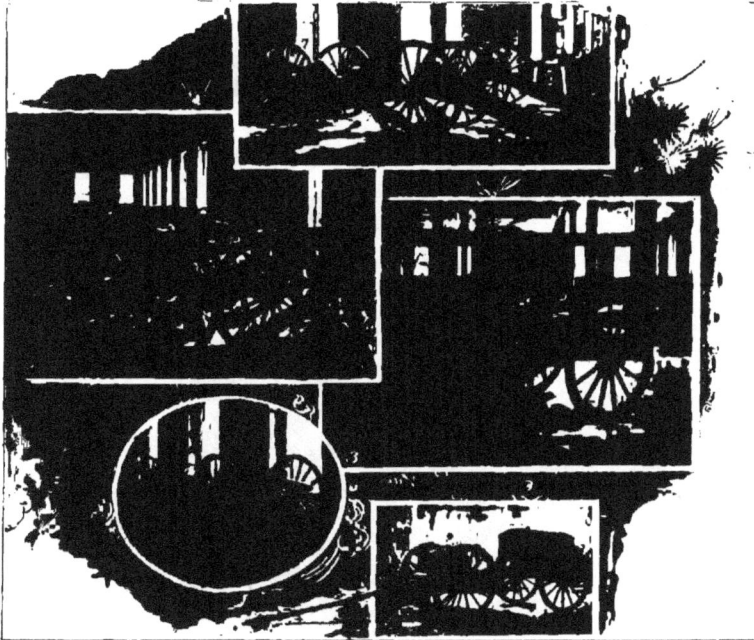

1. Field-Gun Carriages in Shop.
2. Gatling Guns.
3. Gatling Gun.
4. Double-Seated Field Gun.
5. Battery Wagon.

the entire military and naval establishment. New and distant territory has been acquired, both by conquest and annexation, and this must be fortified and guarded. Serious questions have arisen and must arise, and they can only be answered by preparation. There is no escape from the heavy responsibilities that have come uninvited and unexpected. Differences of opinion may exist on how best to solve the problems, but there can be none on the urgency of preparation for defense.

## THE FIRST ARSENAL.

In the first war the Colonies had neither arsenals nor armories, but in the very year of their independence the States began the manufacture of powder, and a year later (1777) brass cannon were cast in Philadelphia. An arsenal was established at Carlisle, Pennsylvania, and a foundry and laboratory were, on the recommendation of Washington, begun at Springfield, Massachusetts. This was the origin of

COMMANDANT'S HOUSE AND GROUNDS.

1. The Residence.
2. The Shaded Lawn.
3. The Garden and Greenhouse.
4. Summer House on the River Bank.
5. The Gateway.

the present National Armory there. Before 1787 the manufacture of small arms had begun. The arsenal at Harper's Ferry was commenced in 1795. These two arsenals furnished small arms and supplies during the War of 1812.

In 1838 the Ordnance Department was placed in charge of the arsenals and armories, of which there were twenty-three in the United States at the beginning of the Civil War. Some of these were small; others were intended only for repairs, and still others merely as depositories. Wisdom came from experience, and in place of the limited and widely scattered arsenals, it was determined to concentrate the work of arming, equipping and supplying the army. Hence, there are now only five principal manufacturing arsenals in the United States.

## SPRINGFIELD ARMORY.

This is located on the Connecticut River, in southern central Massachusetts. Since the abandonment of Harper's Ferry Armory, Springfield has been the only manufactory for small arms—rifles, carbines and swords for the army. The Springfield rifle, which for so many years was carried by the soldiers, takes its name from this place, where it was gradually developed to its present perfection. This arm was replaced, four or five years ago, by the United States magazine rifle and carbine, and that gun has since been manufactured at Springfield Armory. Before the war, the average rate of production was slightly over 100 guns a day. This was greatly increased by the addition of a number of machines, until about 320 guns are now being turned out daily, or rather were a few weeks ago. The maximum number of employes at Springfield was reached in the month of July, 1898, when it was slightly over 1,900, with a pay roll for that month of about $125,000. Further additions to the plant have lately been made, and it is expected that before the close of the year it will be possible to turn out 400 guns each day. Springfield Armory is in two parts, separated by about a mile. At one, known as the Water shops, the heavy forging is done; the parts are then transferred to what is known as the Hill shops, which comprise three large buildings about 300 by 60 feet, each with three floors which are well filled with machinery. There are no railway conveniences for transferring between the two parts of the armory, and this has to be done by teaming through the Springfield streets.

It can readily be seen how many economies could be exercised if small arms manufacture were, at least some of it, transferred to Rock Island, with its vacant shops admirably arranged and all ready for the necessary plant.

## FRANKFORD ARSENAL.

This is located in the suburbs of Philadelphia. It has been established many years and is now the principal manufactory of projectiles for the army. None of its buildings are particularly modern, nor are they so well arranged as new ones would be which had been designed particularly for the purpose to which they are now put.

47

## WATERTOWN ARSENAL.

This establishment is in the city of Watertown, just outside Boston. It is one of the older arsenals, but its development to its present capacity has only been of recent years. It is the main manufactory of the huge steel carriages for the large guns used for coast defense, corresponding in that respect to the field and siege carriages now made at Rock Island Arsenal. Watertown's principal output is the Buffington-Crozier gun carriage for 8, 10 and 12 inch rifles. The Arsenal is entirely incapable, however, of producing the number of these required for the service, and the greater part are being made under contract by different private establishments throughout the country.

BATTERY IN ACTION.
Firing a National Salute on the Fourth of July.

## WATERVLIET ARSENAL.

This post is located on the west side of the Hudson River, opposite the city of Troy. Its shops have been almost entirely rebuilt within the last ten years. The principal building is the great gun factory, which is nearly 1,000 feet long and 130 feet broad. It is filled from one end to the other with enormous lathes, boring machines, sharpeners, presses, etc., required in the manufacture of our huge seacoast cannon. As the largest of these guns is over fifty feet long and weighs about 110,000 pounds, the size of the necessary machines for its fabrication can be imagined. Recently the necessary machine tools for the manufacture of the 16-inch guns, which, manifestly, must exceed the size and weight of those just previously mentioned, have been added to the shops, and one of the guns is now in process of fabrication. The manufacture of seacoast cannon is a process which cannot be hastened, and from the first boring and turning of the various parts, and their heating and assembling in the shrinkage, of their rifling, etc., must all be conducted with due deliberation; also the immense amount of care and refinement, far greater than that required in the great majority of machine shops. Many men, therefore, cannot be employed, and though the shop has been pushed to its capacity of running twenty hours a day during the recent war, it has not partaken of the stir and bustle and rush which have been so noticeable features of the recent operations at Rock Island Arsenal.

## BENICIA ARSENAL.

To the four arsenals named must be added that of Benicia, about twenty miles from San Francisco. Some little repair work necessary to put in good condition any broken or unserviceable parts of the equipment of the Pacific Coast is done at that place, but it is in no sense a manufacturing arsenal.

## OTHER ARSENALS, DEPOTS AND STOREHOUSES.

There are several depots which, during the Civil War of thirty-five years ago, were used as manufactories, but no longer have a modern plant and are not capable of very much work. Some of these, however, during the war with Spain, have been running on equipment work for the infantry and cavalry soldier in conjunction with that done at Rock Island. At Allegheny Arsenal, Pittsburg; Columbia, Tennessee, and San Antonio, Texas, operations have been conducted on blanket bags and their straps, haversacks and straps, saddles, bridles and halters. In all these cases the material had been partly fabricated into the desired article at Rock Island Arsenal, and then sent to these establishments for completion. This became necessary to relieve the pressure at Rock Island, the plant not being adequate to fully complete all the stores.

Fort Monroe Arsenal, at Fort Monroe; New York Arsenal, in New York Harbor; Kennebec Arsenal, at Augusta, Maine, and Augusta Arsenal, at Augusta, Georgia, are the remaining arsenals of the country. They are mainly storehouses for the reception and distribution of the outputs of the other arsenals, and are in no sense manufacturing establishments.

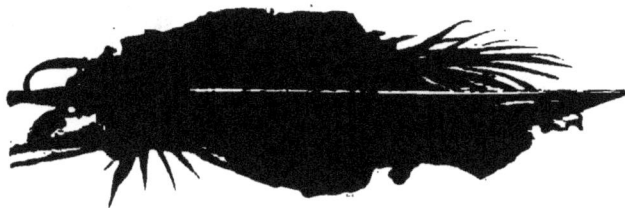

OFFICER'S SWORD.

49

# ROCK ISLAND ARSENAL.

---

The Arsenal designed for the manufacture of the carriages, implements and equipments, and harness for both field and siege artillery, is the Rock Island Arsenal. It is the one that is best suited for this work.—*Report of General Flagler, Chief of Ordnance, to Secretary of War, October 1, 1896.*

Economy dictates the advantage of manufacturing all our field and siege carriages at this Arsenal. Ample and most excellent shops were completed many years ago for this purpose, and are available. — *Report of General Flagler, Chief of Ordnance, to Secretary of War, October 1, 1897.*

THE act of Congress locating the National Arsenal on Rock Island was approved July 11, 1862, and it appropriated for that purpose $100,000. This was the first action of Congress looking definitely to the building of the Arsenal.

Ground for the first building — that now so prominent at the west end of the Island, but in fact only a storehouse and really no part of the active Arsenal — was broken September 1, 1863. The tower of this building is supplied with a large clock, whose face can be seen and whose striking can be heard at a great distance. The dial is twelve feet in diameter.

A REAR VIEW OF SHOP B, NORTH SIDE.

## THE MASSIVE SHOPS.

The row of five shops south of the main avenue is for the Arsenal, and the five north of the same avenue are for the Armory. The center shop in each row is the forging shop and foundry of the Arsenal, and the other four are designed for finishing wood, leather and metal working of all kinds, specially for the manufacture of all the material of war. The center shop of the north row is the rolling mill and forging shop for the Armory, and the two shops on either side of it are finishing and woodworking or "stocking" shops for the manufacture of all kinds of small arms. The center shop in each row is only one story high, and the other four have a basement and three stories. The ground plans of all the ten shops are alike. Each building consists of two parallel wings, 60 by 300 feet, 90 feet apart. This leaves an interior court 90 by 238 feet. The porticos at the sides project 12 feet, and are 60 feet wide, and those in front project 2 feet and are also 60 feet wide. The total area of each shop, including thickness of walls, is 44,280 square feet — a little more than one acre.

The walls of these buildings are entirely of stone. The exterior or face stones are heavy ashlar, laid in courses, jointed, and having a squarely broken face, without tool marks. The backing is rubble, laid also in courses, and has its face, which forms the interior of the wall, well pointed. The average thickness of the walls is as follows : First story, 3 feet 4 inches ; second story, 2 feet 10 inches ; third story, 2 feet 4 inches. The amount of material entering into the construction of one of these buildings is enormous. In shop A, the first built, for instance, there are 30,115,800 pounds of rock, 26,000 of copper, 362,500 of slate, 1,331,500 of lumber, 2,199,646 of iron, 3,132,800 of brick, 200,000 of plaster.

These shops are not only the largest and best for arsenal and armory purposes in the United States, but they are hardly equaled in the world. No other arsenal

in this country even approaches Rock Island in its spacious, solid, costly and endur-
ing buildings. In the rear of three of these shops are fireproof stone storehouses.
And of corresponding modern completeness are the barracks for six families and 170
men, the commanding officer's quarters, the subaltern officers' quarters, the general
offices and fire-engine house.

One powder magazine has been completed, though it is not intended that any
considerable amount of powder will ever be stored at the Arsenal. Safety demands
that it should be stored at the regular powder depots.

# WHAT THE ARSENAL HAS COST.

A question of material value, and one that it has not been easy to correctly answer, is this: "What has Rock Island Arsenal cost?" The investment covers a period of thirty-six years, and there is actual and full value to show for it, the appropriations for preservation and production of supplies and equipments not being included in the following recapitulation of cost of construction work from 1863 to September, 1898:

| | CONSTRUCTION OF BUILDINGS AND OTHER ARSENAL WORK. | ROCK ISLAND WATER POWER. | ROCK ISLAND BRIDGE. | MACHINERY AND SHOP FIXTURES. | TOTALS. |
|---|---|---|---|---|---|
| Under Maj. C. P. Kingsbury, 1863-1864 . . . . | $  231,384.72 | ——— | ——— | ——— | $  231,384.72 |
| Under Gen. T. J. Rodman, 1864-1871. . . . . | 1,855,455.62 | $440,506.35 | $  6,664.33 | ——— | 2,302,626.30 |
| Under Gen. D. W. Flagler, 1871-1886 . . . . . | 4,137,675.24 | 591,911.47 | 160,894.74 | $92,000.00 | 4,982,481.45 |
| Under Col. T. G. Baylor, 1886-1889 . . . . . . . . | 201,200.00 | 322,000.00 | 96,250.00 | 44,000.00 | 663,450.00 |
| Under Col. J. M. Whittemore, 1889-1892 . . . . | 69,000.00 | 101,000.00 | 182,318.48 | 25,000.00 | 377,318.48 |
| Under Col. A. R. Buffington, 1892-1897 . . . . . | ——— | 67,500.00 | 315,125.50 | 50,000.00 | 432,625.50 |
| Under Maj. S. E. Blunt, 1897-1898 . . . . . . . . | 1,500.00 | 73,150.00 | 28,375.00 | 98,627.20 | 201,652.20 |
| Totals . . . . . . | $6,496,215.58 | $1,596,067.82 | $789,628.05 | $309,627.20 | $9,191,538.65 |

1.  THE NEW MAGAZINE RIFLE.     2.  THE CAVALRY CARBINE.     3.  SPRINGFIELD RIFLE.

THE GOVERNMENT WATER POWER.

1. The Big Line Shaft.     2. Dynamo Room.     3. Putting Cable on a Tower.
4. Wire Transmission.     5. Main Cable Driving Wheel.

# THE GREAT WATER POWER.

The low-water flow of the Mississippi River here is 26,000 cubic feet per second ; the high-water flow is 251,000 cubic feet per second; the average flow is 62,000 cubic feet per second. Using the low-water flow of the river, about all of which will be available, we have 45,500 gross horse-power, the second largest water power in the world, Niagara Falls ranking first.

Here, 384 miles below St. Paul, there are rapids over a succession of rocky chains extending across the river, and the descent is 20.4 feet in a distance of 14.75 miles. The rapids consist of a series of pools alternating with rapids over rock in place, which crosses the river in a series of dams; these are called chains, and there are ten such designated on the United States Engineer's maps.— *Extracts from an Address by E. W. Boynton, City Engineer of Davenport, before the Western Waterways Convention, held in Davenport, October 5 and 6, 1897.*

EXPERIENCED engineers from the early days of sixty years ago and more, when Lieut. Robert E. Lee and others made surveys of the Rock Island Rapids, up to this time, have remarked the great available water power that the fall in the Mississippi River furnishes at all stages. The economic value of this power, so long acknowledged, has been intensified during the past decade that has witnessed such wonderful advances in our knowledge and application of electricity. The Rock Island Rapids water power is more than a possibility — it is an actuality ; one that runs giant machines in the Arsenal shops and in the cities of Moline, Rock Island and Davenport; one that turns night into day by its illumination; one that makes this locality great as an industrial center, and one that must make it much greater in the

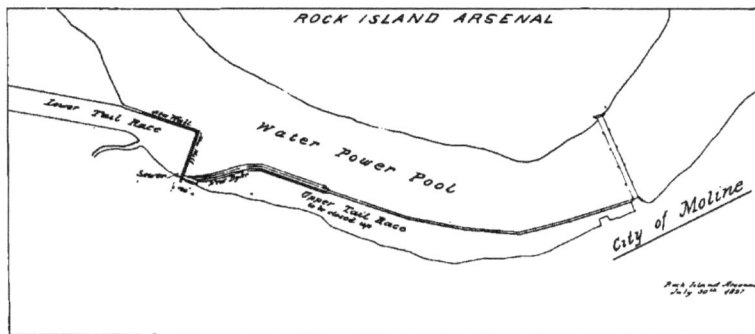

NEW WATER-POWER DAM.

(The two wings are 192 and 208 feet long, respectively, with a heavy triangular pier at the angle. There are twenty-five wheel openings — twelve in one wing and thirteen in the other.)

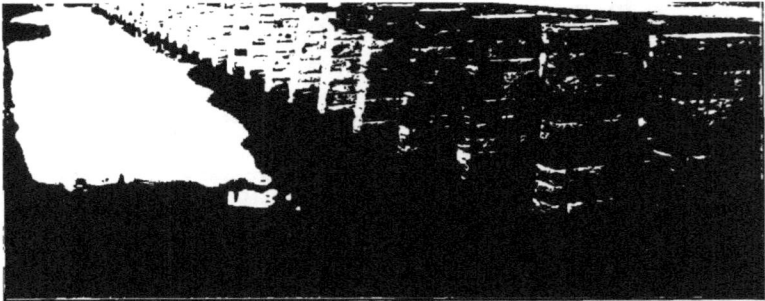

GOVERNMENT WATER-POWER DAM, FROM BELOW.

near future. Water power, both developed and undeveloped, is the prized possession of this busy community.

This water power, as has been shown in the extract at the head of the chapter,
is almost unlimited. On it the United States Government has constructed dams and
gates which make ready for use as wanted nearly 4,000 horse-power. The Moline
Water Power Company will have, when the improvements now under way are completed, thirty gates in their dam. They have modern wheels, each of which gives
them 100 horse-power with an ordinary 6½ or 7 foot head of water, or they have
altogether a developed horse-power of 3,000.

The Arsenal has forty openings in its fine dam, and eight of these openings
have wheels in them. The Government, therefore, has at its command for supplying
the Arsenal with motive power, when the thirty-two wheels are put in, a capacity of
4,000 horse-power, as stated. The improvements in progress, for which contracts
were let last August, consist in running a water-tight dam from the Duck Creek chain
of rapids down the river until it meets the present Arsenal wing dam above the head
of the Island, with the anticipated effect, instead of having the head of the water
obtained from the east end of the Island down, of getting that from the Duck Creek
chain westward. This, at low stage of water, it is expected, will add about 2½ feet
to the head and from twenty-five to fifty per cent to the available water power at the
dams.

56

# THE ARSENAL IN PEACE.

To be prepared for War is one of the most effectual means of preserving Peace.— *Washington to Congress, January 8, 1790.*

SINCE General Lee surrendered to General Grant, the commander of the Union army, on April 9, 1865, at Appomattox Courthouse, Virginia, the country has been at peace. The energy and wealth of the people have for thirty-three years been closely directed to developing the marvelous resources of the Nation. So intent were the people in pursuing the arts of industry, commerce and agriculture that they forgot the axiom of the old philosopher, "We should provide in Peace what we need in War," and the more modern truth of " Eternal Vigilance."

HEADQUARTERS BUILDING.

Congress has been asked time and again by officials of the army and navy to make more liberal appropriations for equipment and defense, in view of an emergency that might suddenly confront the country. Repeatedly has the Chief of Ordnance, Gen. D. W. Flagler, pointed out the urgent necessity, in the interests of economy as well as of defense, for more money with which to provide the empty shops at Rock Island Arsenal with machinery.

But the country had fallen into a state of overconfidence and unwarranted security. From this it was suddenly aroused when, on April 25, 1898, formal declaration of war was recommended by President McKinley, and a bill declaring that "war exists between the United States of America and the Kingdom of Spain" passed both houses of Congress.

Quickly came the calls for 125,000 volunteers ; for 75,000 more volunteers, and for immunes. The force of the regular army was largely increased, and in a few weeks the little organization of less than 25,000 effective men was enlarged to 278,500. The navy was strengthened. Battleships were bought wherever they

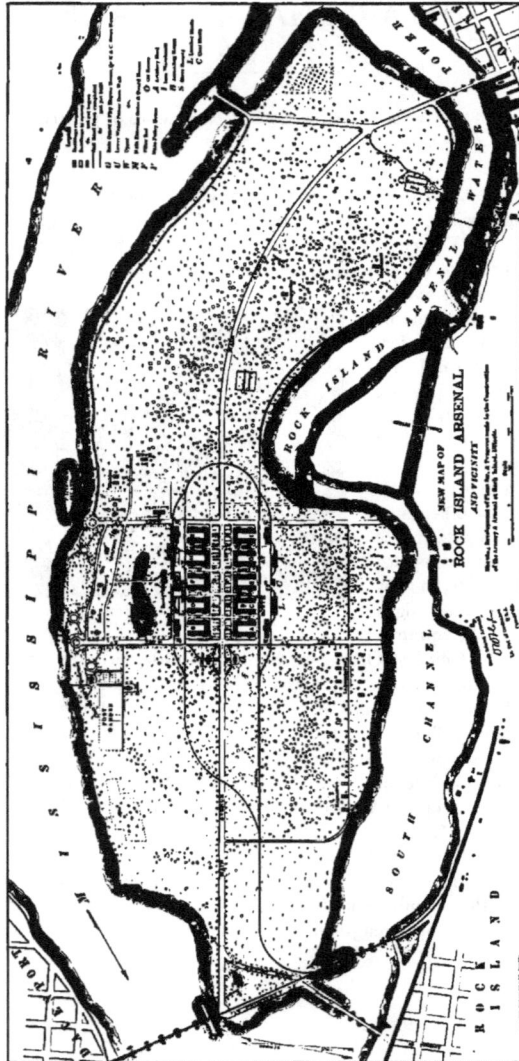

NEW MAP OF
ROCK ISLAND ARSENAL
AND VICINITY

could be found, and old hulks, to be later sunk, were pressed into the service. The volunteers were ready, and the available maximum of 10,000,000 men for military duty was in reserve. Hundreds of millions of dollars were offered the Government. But with all these magnificent "sinews of war," there was delay; costly, impatient and dangerous waiting. The willing soldiers could not be equipped, and they were not

ASSISTANT OFFICERS' QUARTERS.

for nearly three weary months. The great Washington's injunction had been disregarded. War came, and the country was not prepared for it; and a cessation of hostilities followed after 114 days, given to "getting ready" rather than to fighting, so far as the army was concerned. Had the foe been a stronger power, what in reason would have been the consequences?

What Rock Island Arsenal has done in time of peace, owing to the inaction of Congress, is far below what it might and ought to have been. It has slowly added to its machinery and men, and its output has been steadily increased, but not at a rate equaling the Nation's progress in other directions.

The history of the Arsenal for the past eight years is told officially in the following extracts from the reports of the Chief of Ordnance to the Secretary of War, and in those of the commanding officer:

[*From the report of the Chief of Ordnance, October 10, 1890.*]

The manufacture of equipments for the infantry, cavalry and artillery soldier, the horse equipments for cavalry and the artillery harness has been transferred to the Rock Island Arsenal. This transfer, while largely increasing the force of workmen and manufactures at Rock Island, will afford much needed space at Watervliet for the accessories of gun-making.

STOREHOUSE A.
(Located at the foot of the Island, and the only one of the Arsenal buildings in full view of passing trains.)

59

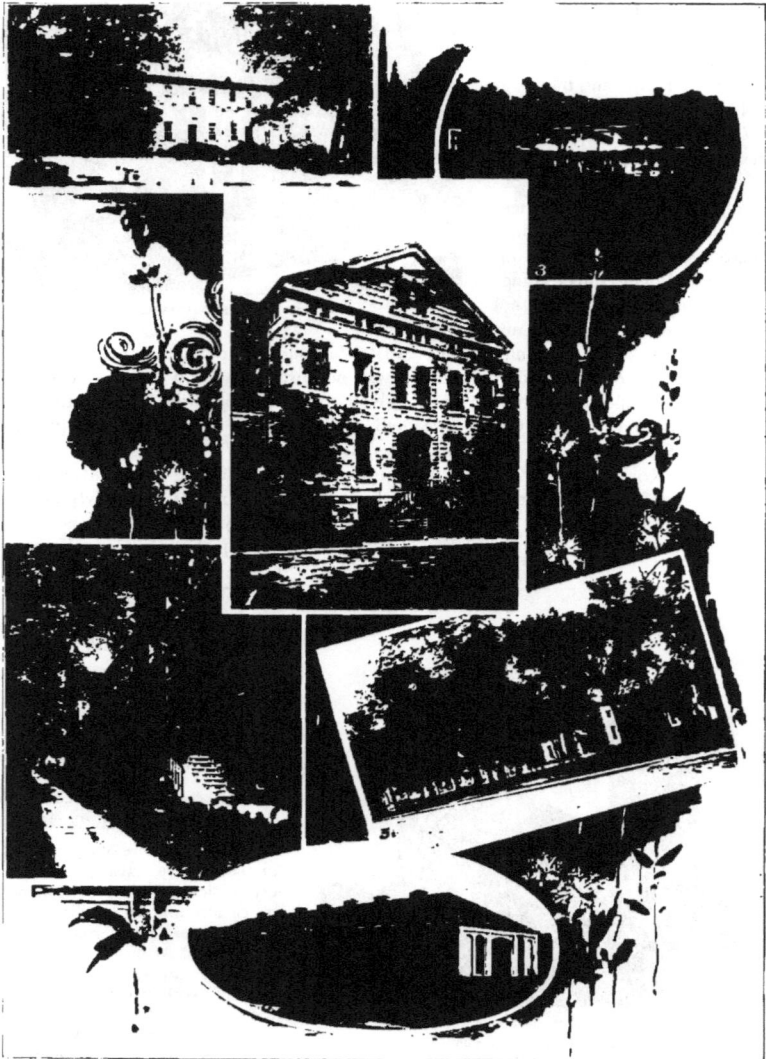

1. ELEVATION OF A SHOP'S SIDE PORTICO.
2. THE OLD HOSPITAL.
3. A POWDER MAGAZINE.
4. ALONGSIDE SHOP A.
5. QUARTERMASTER'S OFFICE.
6. LUMBER DRY-HOUSE.

A further transfer of manufactures from other arsenals, including field carriages and implements, is contemplated to be made to the Rock Island Arsenal in order to concentrate there as much work as is consistent with the best interests of the public service.

*[From the report of the Chief of Ordnance, October 1, 1891.]*

It is expected at an early date to utilize some of the excellent and extensive facilities of this Arsenal for manufactures by transferring the construction of field and siege carriages and the equipments therefor, and some other manufacturing work, to this Arsenal.

THE BARRACKS.
1. Front View.          2. Rear View.

*[From the report of Capt. M. W. Lyon, commanding Rock Island Arsenal, June 30, 1891.]*

During the year the equipment plant of Watervliet Arsenal has been transferred here, and all the work formerly done there is now included in our manufactures. The standard of work turned out has improved, and no complaints of any kind have been heard by us.

*[From the report of the Chief of Ordnance, October 1, 1892.]*

The manufacture of field and siege artillery carriages has been transferred to Rock Island Arsenal, and the plant therefor is being established. The manufacture of nearly all equipments for the army is already established at this Arsenal.

SYLVAN WATER, OPPOSITE MOLINE.

*[From the report of the Chief of Ordnance, October 1, 1893.]*

The necessary work required for placing old and new machinery in other shops has been progressing rapidly, with a view to preparing for the additional output required of this Arsenal.

*[From the report of the Chief of Ordnance, October 1, 1894.]*

The plant for the manufacture of field and siege artillery carriages inaugurated at Rock Island Arsenal two years since is now in active operation. It is organized for the construction of: (1) machine-gun carriages; (2) field-gun carriages, steel, for 3.2-inch breech-loading field guns; (3) limbers, caissons, battery wagons and forges for 3.2-inch breech-loading field guns; (4) carriages and limbers for 5-inch breech-loading siege guns and 7-inch breech-loading howitzers.

The equipment of the infantry, cavalry and artillery services are largely supplied from this Arsenal. * * * More machinery is needed and should be added for more economical work.

*[From the report of the Chief of Ordnance, October 1, 1895.]*

All infantry and cavalry equipments, artillery harness, target materials, and other similar supplies for the use of the army and the militia, are manufactured at Rock Island Arsenal, and this work has been satisfactorily performed during the year to the extent of the appropriations available therefor.

The field and siege gun carriages and implements for our artillery service are manufactured at this Arsenal.

*[From the report of the Chief of Ordnance, October 1, 1896.]*

The work to be carried on in the various departments at the Rock Island Arsenal included the completion of fifty 3.2-inch field-gun carriages, with their limbers complete; twenty 5-inch siege-gun carriages, and twelve 7-inch howitzer carriages.

The receipts at this post from the army, with smaller lots from the militia and sundry persons, consisted of 780 lots, weighing about 550,000 pounds, and the issue, principally to the army, amounted to 1,894 lots, aggregating in weight 1,300,000 pounds.

The Arsenal designed for the manufacture of the carriages, implements and equipments, and harness for both field and siege artillery, is the Rock Island Arsenal. It is the one that is best suited for this work. All of these carriages are of steel and are of new types, and the requirements admit of only the highest excellence in the character of work that it is possible to obtain.

The plans contemplate the ultimate addition to this plant of all the machines that Shop G can accommodate, for use in times of emergency, and it is believed that the shop has sufficient capacity, when so utilized in connection with such work as could still be performed in the general machine shop, to make the annual output about 240 field carriages, 360 caissons, 40 combined battery wagons and forges, 30 traveling carriages and limbers for the 5-inch siege guns, 30 carriages and limbers for the 7-inch siege howitzers and 30 carriages for the 7-inch siege mortars.

A BILL OF GOODS.

[*From the report of the Chief of Ordnance, October 1, 1897.*]

During the fiscal year the infantry equipments, cavalry accouterments, horse equipments, material for target practice, artillery harness, field and siege carriages, caissons, battery wagons and forges, and many other articles required by the army, colleges and militia, have been manufactured at Rock Island Arsenal, and most of the issues to the army, colleges and militia have been made direct from this Arsenal. The construction of the field and siege carriages, with their limbers, caissons and battery wagons and forges, has also been pushed at this Arsenal to the extent that the limited plant available for this work would permit, for the accumulation of the reserve of these carriages that will be required for immediate issue in case of emergency.

[*From the report of Capt. S. E. Blunt, commanding Rock Island Arsenal, July 31, 1897.*]

The manufactures at Rock Island Arsenal during the year (1896-97) have been of two general classes, the various articles of infantry equipments, cavalry accouterments, horse equipments and other similar ordnance stores, which were made to a value of $235,571, and field-gun carriages, limbers, caissons, battery wagons and forges, 5-inch siege carriages, 7-inch howitzer carriages, siege limbers, with the necessary implements and equipments for the artillery service and repairs to the same, and to Gatling-gun carriages and limbers, all to a value of $182,713, or a total value for articles manufactured of $418,285.

In addition, a large amount of work was done on field and siege carriages, which are still in hand. The force employed, which was considerably increased during the last months of the fiscal year, numbered 550 employes of all grades at its close.

ARSENAL WORKMEN LEAVING FOR HOME.

# THE ARSENAL IN WAR.

The efficient work done at Rock Island Arsenal during the few months of the late war with Spain has more than returned, in advantage to the country, the great cost of its construction.—*Hon. W. B. Allison, Chairman, Senate Committee on Appropriations.*

IT has been the unchanged intention of the War Department and of Congress, since 1862, to make Rock Island Arsenal, in the words of General Benet when he was Chief of Ordnance, "the grand ordnance manufacturing establishment in the Mississippi Valley, with larger capacity when completed than any other Arsenal within our borders."

The broad plans that have been so well laid, when fully completed and the shops are crowded to their capacity, look to the arming, equipping and supplying of an army of 750,000 men. It is estimated that the capacity of this Arsenal will be, finally, from two and one-half to three times that of all the arsenals the United States had during the Civil War, and fully equal to all the necessities of the Northwest and the

FOUNDRY AND ROLLING MILL.

Mississippi Valley, from the Alleghanies on the east to the Rockies on the west.

An approach to a realization of this grand design has been made during the war of this year with Spain. Like magic the incomplete Arsenal responded to the heavy demands made upon it. It should be borne in mind that while not more than one-fifth the floor space is supplied with the special machinery required, Rock Island Arsenal has been first of all the arsenals in the United States in the magnitude of the work performed, in the great variety of product, in the number of employes and in the aggregate of wages paid in a single month.

In the respects named, in the large size and substantial character of the buildings, and also in the area of the military reservation containing the Arsenal, Rock Island stands preëminently first.

## VARIETY OF PRODUCTS.

At this Arsenal all the numerous articles that go to make up the equipment of the infantry, cavalry and artillery soldier, with the single exception of his arms, are fabricated. The blanket bag, with its straps, in which the soldier carries the articles of clothing which are kept about his person; the haversack, intended for his rations; the canteen, fashioned from sheet tin and covered first with felt and then with a heavy thickness of duck, which the soldier uses for his water supply or for carrying his coffee between camps; the meat can, a most ingenious device, part frying pan, part plate, with the handle which secures all the parts together, are made here; also the tin cup, used as a coffee boiler, which by its handle can be carried conveniently, secured to the haversack. Knives, forks and spoons used in the mess equipment are also furnished from here; and the bayonet scabbards, made in the rough at other arsenals, are sent to Rock Island to be finished with the leather frogs and the swivel, and large brass hook which permits the soldier to carry them.

The cavalry and horse equipment, comprising first the saddle, made from the raw lumber through its different operations of planing, cutting into length, trimming in the band saw, giving finished shape on the eccentric turner, and finally smoothing and preparing for the assembling of the completed tree, are all performed here. The tree, afterward covered, first with rawhide and then with leather, is then furnished with the necessary rings, hooks and straps for carrying the cavalryman's many articles. Carbine scabbards, great leather pouches fastened to the saddle and forming the receptacle for the carbine when the soldier is mounted; saddlebags, which for the cavalryman serve the same purpose as the blanket bag of the infantry soldier, are made out of leather and provided with the necessary conveniences for carrying them on the cantle of the saddle; surcingles, curb bridles, watering bridles, halters and their straps, lariats, picket pins, nose bags, horse brushes, currycombs, all from their names sufficiently specifying their use, are also a part of the output of this Arsenal. Pistol holsters,

THE STEAM HAMMER.

66

GROUP OF DAY FOREMEN.

spurs and straps, saber belts and plates, the saber knots and other articles of the cavalryman's equipment are likewise produced at Rock Island, besides hundreds more of comparatively minor importance.

## FIELD AND SIEGE GUN CARRIAGES.

In the preceding chapter on "The Arsenal in Peace" it has been shown from the official reports of the Chief of Ordnance how the variety of work has been extended during the past few years. The need of the partial preparation has been more than demonstrated by the shipments to the front during the past few months. Reference is made to the manufacture of the 3.2-inch field carriage, with its limber and caisson, its battery wagon and forge ; and also the carriage and limber for the 7-inch howitzer and for the 5-inch siege gun. These are made of steel, forged and fashioned to shape under hammers and presses, and finally assembled into the finished

1. FOR PEACE OR WAR.
2. FRYING PAN.
3. DOUBLE-WEB BELT.
4. SADDLEBAGS.
5. INFANTRYMAN'S EQUIPMENT.
6. A BLANKET.
7. CAVALRYMAN'S EQUIPMENT.

article. To these are also added the most innumerable articles forming a part of a battery equipment — the sponges, priming wires, sights, anvils, lanterns. To continue the enumeration would be almost equal to taking an inventory of a hardware store. Artillery harness for these batteries is made here, with its great number of spare parts issued to the service.

## A GREAT WORKSHOP FOR REPAIRS.

Besides the regular fabrications, the Arsenal is a great workshop for repairs upon all of these stores, first issued to the field and then, after much service, turned in as no longer being quite equal to the work required of them. Here they are again put into shape, worn parts replaced, old parts cleaned where possible, until the article assumes almost the appearance of new.

## A DEPOT OF ISSUE.

The Arsenal is also the greatest depot in the country for the issue of supplies to the army. Much of the ammunition and many of the small arms made elsewhere are sent to Rock Island and from here distributed to the soldier. The receipts and shipments are, therefore, enormous—much more than those of all the other arsenals combined—and the railroad track with its sidings is always well provided with cars.

GROUP OF NIGHT FOREMEN.

| | | | |
|---|---|---|---|
| 1. Chris Pedersen. | 3. Homer Tilton. | 5. J. B. Schoessel. | 7. C. C. Wilson. |
| 2. J. H. Winter. | 4. Samuel Westberg. | 6. H. J. Risley. | 8. W. H. Bragdon. |

The rapidity with which the normal number of employes, about five hundred, was raised to nearly six times that effective force in the emergency of the war hardly needs comment. It demonstrates that the great plant is ready for expansion, and that the output can be increased to almost any extent without confusion. The character of the employes is shown by the quality of their product. Government work is of the highest standard. This cluster of cities, Davenport, Rock Island and

IN THE HARNESS SHOP.

1. General View.   2. Cutting Room.   3. Another View.   4. Canteen Straps.

Moline, is an industrial center, with thousands of artisans, mechanics and other skilled laborers. When the local supply is inadequate, the demand can be quickly met. The plow factories, steel works, axle and wheel shops are the largest and best of their class in the country.

## SOME OFFICIAL FACTS.

The annual report for 1898 of Maj. S. E. Blunt, commandant at Rock Island Arsenal, to the Chief of Ordnance, is one of the most interesting and important ever made from this post. It covers a period of nearly fourteen months, and includes the time of most active operations. It gives exact information on many points not

THE TIN-CUP SHOP.

elsewhere accessible. Permission to use essential parts of this report has been granted, and the facts in the following summary may, therefore, be regarded as entirely trustworthy :

## GROUNDS AND BUILDINGS.

The grounds and roads on the Island have not only been maintained, but much improved and made more attractive. In this regard over two hundred young trees were set out along Main avenue. This avenue throughout its length has been resurfaced with macadam.

## ENORMOUS EXPENDITURES.

The experience of the present war, urges the report, has fully demonstrated that for the proper supervision of the many and varied manufactures of this Arsenal, and for the inspection of material and stores received and issued to the army, more assistant officers are necessary. The magnitude of the operations of the Arsenal, with its 2,900 employes, its day and night shifts, its purchases of material for fabrications of field and siege carriages, and for equipments for artillery, cavalry and infantry soldier, as well as of completed equipments from many contractors, * * * can be briefly summarized by the statement that since April 1, 1898 (to August 15), they have involved expenditures from funds allotted to this Arsenal of over $2,600,000.

It is recommended that quarters be provided for two of these officers.

THE MAIN MACHINE SHOP.

1. A General View.　　2. 400 Horse-Power Engine. Shop C.　　3. Making Field-Gun Carriage Trails.
4. Bed Frames for Caissons — Machine Shop.　　5. Slotter at Work, Shop G.

Major Blunt gives some space to the comparatively new and highly important department of field and siege carriages. The basement and first floor of the west wing of Shop G have been prepared for use as a machine and erecting shop for field carriages, limbers, caissons, battery wagons and forges, and for siege carriages and limbers. He adds:

For these two floors the following machines were purchased and all installed during the winter, with their counters and other subsidiary shafting : Six engine lathes of different sizes, three column shapers, eight upright drill presses, three milling machines, one planer, one horizontal boring and drilling machine, one universal radial drilling machine, one bolt cutter and two tool grinders. The necessary number of machinists' bench vises and grindstones were also procured and placed. * * * To provide additional facilities for rapidly turning out

THE MAIN BLACKSMITH SHOP—INTERIOR.

field and siege carriages, etc., the preparation of the basement and first floor of Shop G for the reception of machinery has recently been extended to include its central portion and the east wing. In the central portion the first floor on its street front will comprise a commodious tool room, extending from wing to wing, and so provided with machine tools that all tool making and repairing will be conducted within its limits. Convenient office and store rooms have been made on the court side of this part of the shop. The basement and first floor of the east wing are now ready for the installation of the machinery which has been ordered under the appropriation made for this purpose at the last session of Congress. Some of the machinery has been delivered, and it is hoped all will be established and in operation before the close of the calendar year.

The plant still remaining in Shop C is sufficient and suitable for a very limited production of field and siege carriages or for repairs upon those that may be turned in from the field. Operated in connection with the larger plant in Shop G, it is estimated an annual output can be reached of about ninety field carriages, ninety caissons and fifteen battery wagons and forges, or fifteen complete six-gun batteries; and in addition about twenty siege carriages, with their limbers. It is believed this is not sufficient for the probable needs of the army and that a further provision should be made for completing the plant on the first floor and basement of Shop G and for its extension into the second floor.

## SMALL ARMS.

Last winter the work was begun of cleaning and repairing a number of Springfield rifles sent to Rock Island Arsenal for that purpose. The necessary plant was established in rather a small way, beginning with an output of about forty guns a day. The demand greatly increased and the work was extended until it occupied the entire front and most of the west wing of Shop D. Late in June eighty-five men and boys turned out about five hundred completed rifles or carbines a day. In July there was an increase to about six hundred rifles a day.

The increase of the number to be repaired from the original 10,000 to nearly 50,000, and from the more moderate output of 100 a day to the 600 finally demanded, also added considerably to expenses for equipment. Up to June 30, when 31,000 had been repaired, the cost per gun for tools and equipment had been about 3 cents, the cost for material used in the work about 3¼ cents, and the labor charges about 61¾ cents, or a total cost of about 68 cents a gun.

IN THE CARPENTER SHOP.

74

The transition of the Arsenal from the ordinary state in time of peace to the activity and rush of war suddenly forced upon the country came without confusion. In a few weeks the normal force of less than 500 employes was increased to more than 2,900. New machinery was installed as new men were added. How the Arsenal met the emergency is described by Major Blunt in these words:

Until this year no canteens had been made at this Arsenal, the surplus left over from the war of 1861-65, when repaired and recovered, being sufficient to meet the ordinary demands of the army. The production of meat cans and tin cups had also been always on a moderate scale. The plant in the tin shop had, therefore, comprised only one power press and one power shears, with several folders and other minor tools. * * * Soon five large presses, one of them back-geared, and one medium and four small presses were added; also two double-

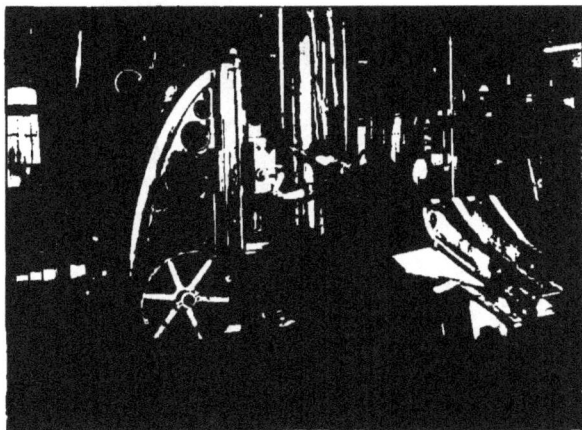

A CORNER IN THE MACHINE SHOP.

seaming machines, two forming rolls, seven burring machines, two wiring machines, one large and one small turner, one beading machine, one groover, four squaring shears, two 30-inch and four 20-inch folders, one setting-down machine, four soldering and two double-seaming stakes, as well as a number of minor tools and appliances, were added.

In the equipment part of the machine shop the plant for the manufacture of buckles, rings, loops, squares, brass hooks of different shapes, saddle irons, ovals and studs, curb bits, snaps, and the many other similar parts of infantry, cavalry and horse equipment, had been based upon the ordinary demands of the army in time of peace, and was entirely inadequate for the immense increase in production so suddenly required from the Arsenal. As for the other shops, the necessary machinery was, however, soon obtained, until fifteen power presses of different sizes, two 3-spindle and one 1-spindle drill presses, two hand milling machines, two 14-inch and two 11-inch speed lathes and a number of different minor bench tools and appliances had been added to the shop equipment. Thirteen additional braziers' furnaces were also

75

THE TIN SHOP.

1. Soldering Canteens.   2. Canvasing Canteens.   3. Putting in Corks.   4. Making Meat-Can Handles.
5. Felt-Covering Canteens.   6. Stack of Covers.   7. Canteens Ready for Covering.

76

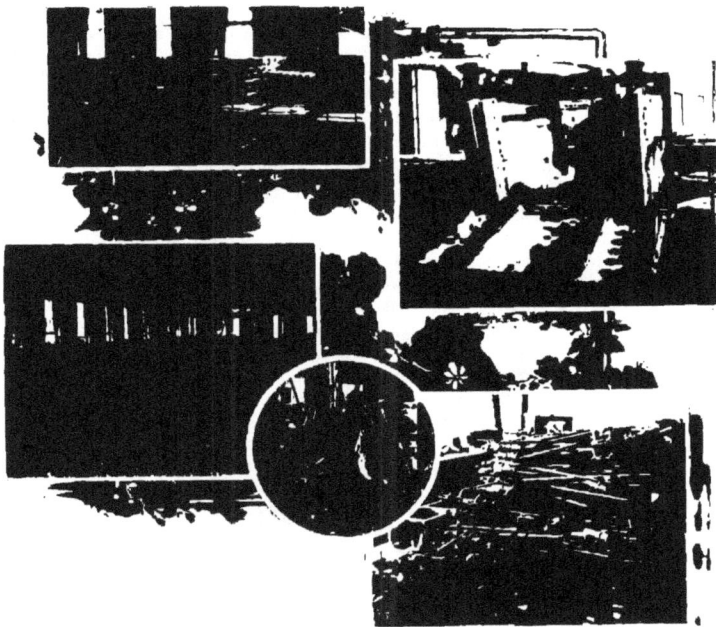

installed, and a 750-gallon Springfield gas machine and a Sturtevant steel-pressure blower to provide the necessary fires.

Increased facilities were likewise added to the blacksmith shop, the foundry and other departments. How this enlarged the output one paragraph from the report will explain :

In the west wing of Shop G nearly four hundred men and boys engaged in sewing, first the felt and afterward the duck covers upon the canteens as made here, or upon those purchased from contractors. The force, as they became more expert, finally reached an output of 8,000 canteens per day. In all, nearly seven hundred men and boys were employed on this floor.

Further details as to how the force was multiplied and the output extended and varied will prove interesting. Major Blunt says :

On March 1, 1898, the usual force of slightly less than five hundred men was employed at the Arsenal, engaged in work upon field carriages and caissons, siege carriages and limbers, and the different articles of infantry equipment, cavalry accouterment and horse equipment which, under the usual orders, had been undertaken earlier. Work was so progressing that all the equipments, based upon the ordinary demands of the army in time of peace, would be completed late in June ; the siege carriages and limbers were nearly finished ; the field-carriage work had only been started a few weeks before.

The record shows that the war which came was anticipated, and, so far as possible, preparations made for it. March 9, General Flagler, the Chief of Ordnance, directed by wire " that work be pushed on all existing orders as rapidly as possible, and that extra shifts of workmen be employed." Steps were promptly taken to comply with instructions, but three days later the telegram of March 9 was partially rescinded. March 26, orders came to manufacture 25,000 sets of infantry equipments, and the number of men was increased to 608 at the end of that month. April 5, orders came in these words : " Press work on all field and siege carriages as rapidly as possible, employing extra shifts of men as far as economical." April 21, instructions were received increasing the infantry equipments to 75,000 sets, and ordering 10,000 sets of horse equipments and 100 sets of artillery harness for led horses. The next day equipment work was put into two shifts, the first of ten hours and the second of eight hours. This a few days later was changed to ten hours for each shift, and work was so continued twenty hours per day until the reductions began, early in August.

SHIPMENTS TO CUBA.

1. A Full Carload.    2. Loading the Carriages.    3. Caissons and Limbers.

78

On May 5, continues Major Blunt, a telegram was received directing me to provide 54,000 sets infantry equipments, 5,000 sets cavalry accoutrements and 5,000 sets horse equipments in addition to those previously ordered, and specifying that they were to be turned out at the rate of 1,500 of the former and 200 of the latter per day, or faster, if possible. I was also advised that the commanding officers of Allegheny, Indianapolis and Columbia arsenals and the master harnessmaker from San Antonio Arsenal would visit this Arsenal to confer with me regarding what fabrications could be advantageously undertaken at their respective ar-

A CORNER IN THE SEWING-MACHINE ROOM.

senals. This conference was duly held, and as a result the manufacture of 30,000 each of blanket, bag, shoulder and coat straps, haversack straps and canteen straps was commenced at Allegheny Arsenal ; of 25,000 blanket bags and straps and haversacks and straps at Indianapolis Arsenal, and also at Columbia Arsenal ; and 3,000 saddles, curb bridles and halters at San Antonio Arsenal. All the buckles, hooks, rings and other similar parts of these equipments were made here and sent to those arsenals ; the duck for blanket bags and haversacks was stamped here and then shipped there. The curb bits for the bridles and the saddletrees were also completed here. Many of the smaller tools were furnished, and also men to serve as foremen.

May 9, telegraphic orders were received for the manufacture of 102 field carriages and limbers, 150 caissons and limbers and 17 battery wagons and forges, and instructions to also procure material for 24 carriages for siege howitzers and for the same number for 5-inch siege guns. June 6, instructions were received to "manufacture or to procure by purchase" 10,000 sets cavalry and horse equipments in addition to previous orders, and that the work be "prosecuted with all possible dispatch." June 15, orders came to make up 3,600 more sets of horse equipments. To meet these "rush" orders it was necessary to let contracts among fifty-two bidders for work to the value of $570,602. June 22, directions were wired to increase what might be called the "mess outfit" part to 5,000 per day, or to 6,000 if it could possibly be done, and steps to reach that number were at once taken. June 25, the manufacture of 148 sets artillery harness for wheel horses was ordered, also 188 sets for led horses ; and on the 27th, instructions to provide 75,000 additional sets of infantry equipments, except certain specified articles. July 7, 12,000 more sets of horse equipments were asked for. These large orders made the calling on contractors imperative for work amounting to $208,087.50. At this time there were forty-six different firms or individuals delivering finished articles of ordnance stores at Rock Island Arsenal, ready, after proper inspection, for issue to troops. The larger part of this order for 12,000 sets of horse equipments it was, however, contemplated to fabricate at this Arsenal, where the facilities for all such work had been very much increased. To quote from Major Blunt's report again :

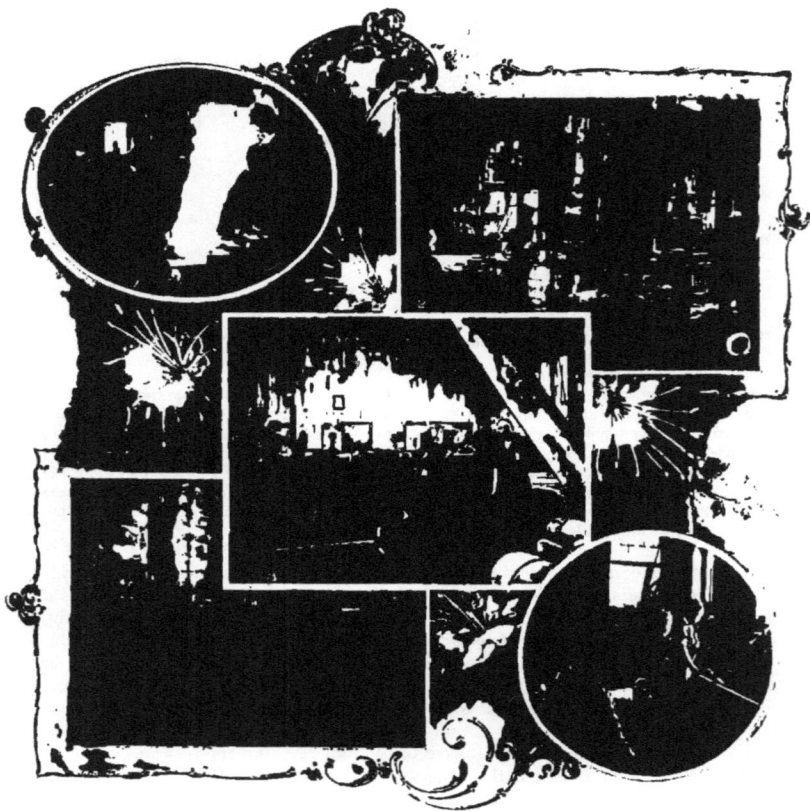

IN THE FOUNDRY.

1. Pouring Off — Brass Foundry.   2. Iron-Melting Furnaces.   3. The Main Molding Room.
4. Old Shells for Recasting.   5. The Brass Molders.

At the close of the war, 131 different firms or individuals were, or had been, delivering material at this Arsenal, and the amounts of some of the principal stores ordered were as follows : 351,400 yards of dyed duck and 1,008,000 yards of cotton webbing, of various widths, for haversacks, blanket bags and canteen covers ; 654,000 pounds of tin plate for meat cans, canteens and tin cups ; 79,900 pounds brass wire and 89,500 pounds of sheet brass for the buckles, rings, hooks, etc., of the different equipments ; 954,000 feet linen rope for lariats ; 205,300 pounds harness-leather backs and 1,262,000 square feet collar, bridle and bag leather for straps, saddles, carbine scabbards, saddlebags, etc.; 116,200 pounds of copper and 1,161,900 pounds of steel and iron for gun carriages, etc., and for the various parts of equipments ; 133,000 feet of basswood and ash for saddletrees, and 690,000 feet of other lumber for ammunition chests, packing boxes, work benches, etc., besides many thousand pounds of minor articles.

No. .........................

**PAY.**

Month of.......

$...................................

A PAY ENVELOPE — EXACT SIZE.

## WAR PERIOD PAY ROLL.

THE NUMBER OF WORKMEN AND AMOUNT OF MONTHLY WAGES AT DIFFERENT PERIODS.

| DATE. | NAMES ON ROLL. | AMOUNT OF MONTHLY ROLL. |
|---|---|---|
| March 31, 1898 . . . . . . . . | 608 | $ 32,708.39 |
| April 30, 1898 . . . . . . . . | 1,077 | 48,789.06 |
| May 31, 1898 . . . . . . . . | 1,784 | 90,179.82 |
| June 30, 1898 . . . . . . . . | 2,312 | 126,659.24 |
| July 31, 1898 . . . . . . . . | 2,902 | 175,030.73 |

It will be observed that in the last three months, when work was being prosecuted more nearly to the capacity of the Arsenal with its present plant, the sum paid in wages to the employés aggregated nearly $400,000.

No difficulty whatever was experienced in securing all the men to whom employment could be given — in fact, the applications far exceeded the vacancies in all grades, from the skilled mechanic to the laborer, and, if the capacity of the plant had so permitted, several times the number actually employed could have been obtained. The single exception to this was in regard to harnessmakers, but even in this case I believe no difficulty would have been experienced if the magnitude of the orders to be ultimately given had been known to me more in advance.

## EFFICIENT EMPLOYES.

As the force was increased, the necessity for foremen and inspectors familiar with the successive operations (for there was no time to teach and develop new men) grew with the expansion of the work. They were found among the old employes, and from their ranks a number of temporary appointments to these positions were made. They proved capable and efficient, and when necessary, as was frequently the case, worked overtime with entire willingness; in fact, the spirit they displayed permeated, with very few exceptions, the entire force, the men being apparently animated by the desire to observe the shop rules and regulations to the best of their ability and to render all possible assistance to the Government in the existing emergency.

Major Blunt in particular commends Mr. George Patterson, master machinist. Mr. Patterson was transferred from Watervliet Arsenal, where he had been the principal assistant foreman in the Armory gun factory while Major Blunt was himself in charge there. Speaking of Master Machinist Patterson, the commandant says:

His experience and abilities have since proved of great value, and with his assistance many modifications in the details of manufacture have been introduced which will considerably diminish both the time and cost of production, especially of gun carriages and similar work, but also of many articles of equipment.

THE CROWDED MAIN AVENUE.

1.  A Morning Scene.                    2.  In the Evening.

82

## THE ARSENAL'S OUTPUT.

The principal articles of ordnance stores, either made at Rock Island Arsenal altogether or in part, and received from contractors between April 15 and August 15, may be tabulated as follows:

| ARTICLES. | TOTAL PROVIDED. | ARTICLES. | TOTAL PROVIDED. |
|---|---|---|---|
| 3.2-inch breech-loading rifles and other field guns, | 25 | Bayonet scabbards, hook attach-ment, | 194,432 |
| Carriages, 3-inch and 3.2-inch breech-loading rifle, | 53 | Blanket bags, | 68,798 |
| Limbers, 3.2-inch and 3.6-inch breech-loading rifle, | 210 | Blanket-bag shoulder straps, pairs, | 88,560 |
| | | Blanket-bag coat straps, pairs, | 71,767 |
| Caissons, 3.2-inch and 3.6-inch breech-loading rifle, | 120 | Canteens, | 259,505 |
| | | Canteen straps, infantry, | 202,162 |
| Combined forge and battery wagon, | 1 | Canteen straps, cavalry, | 27,207 |
| Carriages, 7-inch siege howitzer, | 11 | Gun slings, | 155,885 |
| Various implements and equipments for 3.2-inch and 3.6-inch batteries, | 1,390 | Haversacks, | 143,932 |
| | | Haversack straps, | 152,495 |
| Various implements and equipments for 5-inch and 7-inch batteries, | 705 | Meat cans, | 241,599 |
| | | Tin cups, | 260,248 |
| Miscellaneous artillery implements and equipments, | 914 | Knives, | 210,211 |
| | | Forks, | 184,029 |
| Artillery harness, led-horse, sets, | 479 | Spoons, | 287,923 |
| Artillery harness, wheel-horse, sets, | 148 | Waist-belt plates, | 21,223 |
| Artillery harness, extra parts, | 2,440 | Curb bridles, | 1,051 |
| Springfield carbines, caliber .45, | 17,500 | Bridles, watering, | 20,973 |
| Springfield rifles, caliber .45, | 24,300 | Curb bits, | 4,546 |
| Colt's revolvers, caliber .38, | 23 | Carbine boots, | 7,041 |
| Sabers and swords, | 2,447 | Carbine scabbards, | 20,520 |
| Carbine slings, | 8,085 | Currycombs, | 29,769 |
| Carbine-sling swivels, | 4,626 | Halter headstalls, | 18,333 |
| Cartridge belts, calibers .30 and .45, | 37,325 | Halter straps, | 25,087 |
| Cartridge-belt plates, | 50,444 | Horse brushes, | 20,641 |
| Cartridge boxes, calibers .38 and .45, | 7,069 | Lariats, | 11,588 |
| Pistol holsters, calibers .38 and .45, | 16,151 | Lariat straps, | 30,445 |
| Knapsacks, light artillery, | 150 | Links, | 5,836 |
| Saber belts, cavalry, | 18,880 | Nose bags, | 17,031 |
| Saber attachments, | 16,129 | Picket pins, | 27,335 |
| Saber knots, | 2,377 | Saber straps, | 14,674 |
| Spurs, | 43,307 | Saddles, | 13,801 |
| Spur straps, | 52,324 | Saddlebags, pairs, | 20,262 |
| Waist belts, | 11,317 | Side lines, | 2,848 |
| | | Saddle blankets, cavalry and artillery, | 30,732 |

## STORES RECEIVED AND ISSUED.

During the first nine months of the fiscal year (beginning July 1, 1897), the usual amount of infantry equipments, cavalry accouterments, horse equipments, materials for target practice, artillery harness, carriages, caissons, projectiles and powder, small-arm ammunition and many other articles of ordnance stores were issued to the regular army, to colleges and to the militia, and a great quantity of similar articles in an unserviceable condition were turned in here for the repairs necessary to make them again fit for issue.

INTERIORS OF SHOPS.

1. The Paint Shop.　　2. An Attic.　　3. Caissons and Limbers.　　4. Small-Arms Stores.
5. Tons of Saluting Powder.

During the last quarter of the fiscal year these transactions greatly increased. I have, therefore, in the following table, separately included them, and though not properly belonging to the year, yet, as forming part of the issues of the same war period, have also added a report for July, 1898. The weights are given in pounds.

RECEIPTS OF ORDNANCE STORES FROM REGULAR AND VOLUNTEER ARMY AND MILITIA.

|  | JULY 1, 1897, TO MARCH 31, 1898. | APRIL 1, 1898, TO JUNE 30, 1898. | TOTAL FOR YEAR. | JULY, 1898. |
|---|---|---|---|---|
| In less than carload lots . . . | 542,720 | 256,857 | 799,577 | 192,796 |
| In carload lots . . . . . . . | . . . . . . . | 1,008,083 | 1,008,083 | 125,059 |
| Totals . . . . . . . . . | 542,720 | 1,264,940 | 1,807,660 | 317,855 |

ISSUES OF ORDNANCE STORES TO REGULAR AND VOLUNTEER ARMY AND MILITIA.

|  | JULY 1, 1897, TO MARCH 31, 1898. | APRIL 1, 1898, TO JUNE 30, 1898. | TOTAL FOR YEAR. | JULY, 1898. |
|---|---|---|---|---|
| In less than carload lots . . . | 1,031,010 | 756,938 | 1,787,948 | 1,286,347 |
| In carload lots . . . . . . . | . . . . . . . | 3,388,128 | 3,388,128 | 436,915 |
| Totals . . . . . . . . . | 1,031,010 | 4,145,066 | 5,176,076 | 1,725,262 |

The total weight of issues and receipts of these finished stores is 6,983,736 pounds for the fiscal year ending June 30, 1898; for the four months from April 1 to July 31 it is 7,451,123 pounds.

Considering so much of the war period as extended from April 1 to July 31, the stores issued to troops aggregated 5,868,328 pounds, or an average of 48,101 pounds per day, Sundays included. This statement of an average hardly permits, however, an accurate judgment of the daily shipments of the Arsenal during its heaviest period. They were much lighter in April than in the following months, and had begun to decrease in the latter part of July. About the middle of June they for days at a time exceeded 120,000 pounds.

## COST OF CONTRACT WORK.

While fairly favorable prices were obtained for the $1,110,000 worth of finished articles of ordnance stores procured under contracts, yet in all cases they exceeded, in some instances considerably so, the cost at which similar stores were at the same time being turned out at the Arsenal.

## ARGUMENTS FOR THE ARSENAL.

Taking different items for comparison, Major Blunt far more than makes good his statement. In the matter of saddles alone there would have been a saving to the Government of about $30,000 if sufficient saddles had been in store at the breaking out of the war, or if the plant at Rock Island Arsenal had permitted their manufacture with the necessary rapidity. And besides this, as the commandant says : "It must also be remembered that the articles obtained by purchase, especially at such a period, as has unquestionably been the case with most of those recently procured under contracts, are often inferior, both in material and workmanship, to those produced in the Government shops. This fact was universally acknowledged by all contractors who visited this Arsenal during the last few months and examined the work in progress." Assuming the cost of purchases to average about 14 per cent, the commandant reasons it "would mean an expenditure of about $150,000 since the declaration of war that with proper facilities for manufacturing at this Arsenal need not have been made."

## UNDEVELOPED CAPACITIES.

Rock Island Arsenal, observes Major Blunt in concluding his report for 1898 to the Chief of Ordnance, " has now a water power sufficient, if properly utilized, for operating all the machinery that could be placed in its shops. It has ten as fine buildings as exist at any arsenal, or as can be found at any private establishment. They are admirably suited to the purpose for which they were erected, yet in only one of the ten has an adequate amount of machinery been installed, and in two others only fractional parts of the shops are occupied.

" As at present equipped, only about one-fifth of the floor space available has been used for machinery and employes, and it is consequently no exaggeration to maintain that the recent output has borne only that proportion to what could have been accomplished if every floor of every shop had been provided with power and machinery and other facilities for the proper prosecution of work.

" What the undeveloped capacities of the Arsenal are can be surmised by considering, with the multiplier suggested, the figures given in a previous summary for its summer's output. Substitute for some of this product, if deemed advisable, other lines of manufacture not yet introduced, but for which the buildings and their surroundings are adapted, and it will be evident that if the capacity of the Arsenal were fully developed, it would easily prove equal to the task of expeditiously and economically producing the equipment for a large army.

" To attain this end considerable sums will, however, be necessary, but, if judiciously expended, no better or, in the long run, more economical use could be made of the public funds."

THE OLD MILL AT THE HEAD OF THE ISLAND.

# THE FUTURE OF THE ARSENAL.

God grants liberty only to those who love it, and are always ready to guard and defend it.—*Daniel Webster.*

I T has been shown by official figures how Rock Island Arsenal promptly met the sudden and enormous demands made upon it during the war with Spain; but vast as the output was then, and varied as the products were, the Arsenal was not taxed to more than one-fourth its capacity when fully completed. No one is more intimately acquainted with the building of the shops or with what they are intended

ONE OF MANY EMPTY ROOMS.

to do than Gen. D. W. Flagler, the commandant from 1871 to 1886, and for the past eight years Chief of Ordnance, United States Army. General Flagler, in answer to questions in regard to his plans for the future of the Arsenal, and in a conversation during his late visit of inspection to the Island, said:

I have in no particular changed my views as to the wisdom of completing Rock Island Arsenal in accordance with my plans at the time I left it in 1886. No new buildings have been commenced since that time, only because appropriations for their construction were not available. The buildings still required to complete the plans are as follows:

Two stone storehouses like A and Storehouse K, already built. These are to be located— Storehouse I at the intersection of South and East avenues, and Storehouse B at the intersection of North and West avenues.

1. GOING TO THE DEPOT.
2. PACKING EQUIPMENT.
3. A STOREHOUSE.
4. AN UPPER FLOOR STOREROOM.
5. CARS READY FOR LOADING.

Three brick storehouses for lumber, iron and steel, and for artillery and artillery projectiles, similar to the lumber storehouse south of Shop C, are to be located in rear of Shops G, H and D. (The location of all the shops, other buildings and avenues are shown on the map of Rock Island Arsenal on page 58.)

Coal sheds for storing and elevated track for dumping coal in rear of Shop E.

A hospital, stables, and about four additional sets of officers' quarters.

Nine additional inexpensive wooden laboratory buildings on the site which has been prepared for laboratories, on the west side of West avenue, on the plateau near Sylvan Water.

There are required not less than two additional ammunition magazines, similar and adjacent to the one already constructed, near Sylvan Water, and about 650 yards west of West avenue.

Two small powder magazines, about midway between East avenue and Moline bridge, but about 500 yards from each other. The location of these is shown on maps of the Arsenal which I have prepared.

GETTING READY FOR WORK.

89

The total estimated cost of these buildings is $465,000. Water wheels, penstocks and fixtures for utilizing the water power and machinery for transmitting the same to the shops are also required. The cost of these depends upon the plans employed.

The utilization of the five Armory shops at an early day is very important. I cannot say that the late war has made the wisdom of utilizing these shops any more apparent, as I think this was impossible. The necessity for the Armory, in connection with our military system of not keeping a large standing army, but of being ready to make one when required, is a plain and perfectly apparent fact. It appears to me that no experience could make it plainer or more apparent. I left at the Arsenal plans and estimates for the machinery for these shops. I should think that, roughly, it would not be much less than $1,250,000.

REPAIRING RIFLES AND CARBINES.

## CAPACITY OF THE ARSENAL.

I have always placed the capacity of the five Armory shops at 2,500 rifles, revolvers or carbines per day. The adoption of magazine arms reduces this estimate, but I still think that by working two shifts of men the output could be made 2,000 per day.

The capacity of the five Arsenal shops south of Main avenue is not easy to state, because of the great variety of manufactures. A part of Forging Shop E, three stories of Shop G, and probably a part of Shop H, would be used for the construction of field and siege carriages and their implements and equipments. The use of a large part of Shop C, as is done now, for repairs, general work and a harness shop would naturally continue. A large part of Shop A, probably all of the three lower stories, is required for the manufacture of field, siege and small-arm ammunition, except that the loading or charging of the same — that is, all operations involving the addition of the powder — would be continued at the laboratory buildings on West avenue, south of Shop A, which have been mentioned. The rest of these buildings, including nearly all of the top stories of four of the shops, are designed for harness and equipment work. They require additions and much fitting up to adapt them for this work, but can be made available. Temporary wooden buildings could be added for this work if necessary, but I think our experience during the past summer shows that this would not be necessary. I think this experience has shown that there would be capacity for turning out, should it be required, 10,000 sets of infantry equipments, and their complement of horse equipments, per day. The manufacture of artillery harness would be carried on in the same shops, but so much time is required for the manufacture of this harness that it would be wise to carry a part of the harness on hand.

Our experience during the past summer shows that the capacity for the manufacture of small-arm cartridges should not be less than half a million per day, and it would be better if it could be three-quarters of a million. The three lower stories are ample for this, and also for the manufacture of the requisite amount of field-artillery ammunition.

.I have not the means at hand of estimating the cost of the machinery and for completing the fitting up of these five shops as proposed here, but do not think it would be much, if any, less than $600,000. The principal item would be for machinery for manufacture of small-arm cartridges, and, next to that, the additional machinery for the manufacture of carriages, and machinery for the manufacture of modern field-artillery ammunition.

The annual report of the Chief of Ordnance to the Secretary of War bears date October 1, 1898. It is a document of far more than ordinary import because it covers the work done during the war with Spain, and makes suggestions and recommendations in the way of providing for the future. In this review General Flagler devotes more attention to Rock Island Arsenal than in any other report that he has made. Following are extracts :

For many years the annual appropriations for these equipments (infantry, cavalry, artillery and horse) have been barely sufficient, with the utmost economy, to meet the annual consumption of the regular army. There was, therefore, only a small supply of these equipments on hand at the commencement of the war.

It has been the plan of the Department to be prepared to manufacture and supply the equipments as fast as armies could be raised. A portion of the Rock Island Arsenal was constructed for this purpose. It is important to determine from our experience in this war whether this plan is feasible for future wants.

Much credit is due to the commanding officer of the Rock Island Arsenal for his vigorous and efficient labor in installing the plant at the Arsenal and providing these equipments. Attention is invited to his report. (The report of Major Blunt, here referred to, will be found on pages 71-86 of this book.) The plant was installed and the number of employes engaged on the work was increased from about 400 on April 13, to about 2,900 on August 31, 1898. On the latter date the department was turning out about 6,000 sets of infantry equipments per day. The work was commenced on April 13, and pushed with all possible dispatch, and in advance of the appropriations made by Congress in the two deficiency bills of May 31 and July 7.

A LONELY WAY.

Funds were not available for enabling the Department to take any action for increasing field artillery for armies taking the field, until April 21, 1898. The number of batteries that could be equipped was absolutely fixed by the number of modern field guns on hand. There were not enough carriages and harness even for these guns, and the manufacture of the carriages and harness was at once commenced at the Rock Island Arsenal, and pushed to the utmost, and the same action was taken in regard to implements and equipments of all kinds at this and other Arsenals.

There was a shortage of harness at the outbreak of the war, but the resources of the Rock Island Arsenal enabled this to be made up rapidly enough to keep pace with the completion of the carriages and caissons.

General Flagler devotes two pages of his printed report to reviewing the work done at Rock Island Arsenal, adding the following comment :

On March 1 the number of employes was something less than 500, while on July 31 over 2,900 employes were engaged at the Arsenal in doing various kinds of work there undertaken. No great difficulty was experienced in securing all men to whom employment could be given, with the single exception of harnessmakers, and, had the magnitude of the orders to be ultimately given been known in advance, it is probable that even these workmen could have been obtained.

Previous reports have been made as to the inadequacy of the post hospital. It is an old frame structure, erected during the Civil War. The inspector-general has reported that this building is "utterly unfit for hospital purposes, and not worth repairing." Estimates have been repeatedly submitted, and are again included this year. It is really a cruelty to place a sick man in this structure.

The supervision of many manufactures at the Arsenal requires more assistant officers. The magnitude of the operations of the Arsenal, with its 2,900 employes, its night and day shifts, purchases of material for artillery, cavalry and infantry soldiers, and the inspection and examination of equipments received from many contractors, has involved since April 1, 1898 an expenditure of over $2,600,000. (This was up to the middle of August.) Additional quarters are required for assistants, and steps should be taken to provide at least two sets of officers' quarters.

A large number of Springfield arms and other ordnance stores have been repaired at the Arsenal.

Perhaps the most interesting feature of the report of the Chief of Ordnance, certainly so to the readers of " ROCK ISLAND ARSENAL : IN PEACE AND IN WAR," is found in his discussion of the Springfield Armory. He says :

The experience of the department during the late war with Spain has emphasized the necessity, frequently pointed out in my reports, of equipping another armory for the manufacture of small arms. The utmost capacity that could be provided at the Springfield Armory would be about two hundred completed arms for each eight hours' work, or about five hundred per day, since only two shifts of ten hours each can be worked with due regard for economy and perfection of work.

A large reserve of magazine rifles should be provided as soon as possible. To this end the armory buildings at Rock Island Arsenal should be utilized. Their equipment with the necessary machinery, which has already been begun, should be pushed to completion and the manufacture of magazine arms commenced.

The capacity of these buildings is sufficient for increasing the daily output to 2,000 magazine arms per day.

# COMMANDANTS AT THE ARSENAL.

'Tis an office of great worth,
And you an officer fit for the place.—*Shakespeare.*

NO Government post in all the United States has been more favored from the beginning in the high character and acknowledged fitness of the officers designated to command it than Rock Island Arsenal. The War Department always has regard for the special qualifications of its officers in particular lines of duty.

## MAJ. C. P. KINGSBURY.

July 27, 1863, Maj. C. P. Kingsbury, Ordnance Department, was assigned to the command of the Arsenal. Under his direction the storehouse at the western end of the Island, the first building of the Arsenal, was constructed. This building is nearly on the site of old Fort Armstrong, and the window frames of the basement are made of oak obtained from the fort. During Major Kingsbury's command, which lasted until June 30, 1865, the military prison was in use. This proved an annoyance, and the commandant had others to contend with of a more or less serious nature — the railroad right of way, the contests of land claimants not the least among them.

GEN. THOMAS J. RODMAN.
Commandant Rock Island Arsenal,
August, 1865, to June, 1871.

## GEN. THOMAS J. RODMAN.

General Rodman succeeded Major Kingsbury, assuming his duties August 3, 1865, and his command continued until his death, June 7, 1871. Of the significance of this appointment General Flagler says:

No better evidence could be desired that the Ordnance Department intended to construct a great Armory and Arsenal at Rock Island than the fact that an officer of such high standing as General Rodman, and one whose services were so valuable to the department in every way, was selected for the command.

General Rodman was a distinguished soldier, a conscientious officer, who rendered to his country invaluable services in war and in peace. He was graduated from the Military Academy in 1841; served at Allegheny Arsenal till 1848. He was in command of the Arsenal in 1854, and of the one at Baton Rouge, Louisiana, in 1855–56. Except while in service in the Mexican War, he devoted much time to experiments in casting heavy guns on hollow cores. His inventions were numerous. The first 15-inch Rodman gun was completed in May, 1860, and attracted close attention in the military world. During the Civil War General Rodman was in command of the Watertown Arsenal. Many 13 and 15 inch Rodman guns were made for the monitors and forts along the coast. He originated the idea of making heavy guns without preponderance at the breech, on which plan all the heavy cast-iron cannon were subsequently constructed in the United States. In March, 1865, he was brevetted lieutenant-colonel, colonel and brigadier-general for his services in the Ordnance Department.

GEN. D. W. FLAGLER, CHIEF OF ORDNANCE.
Commandant Rock Island Arsenal, 1871 to 1886.

It was February 7, 1866, that General Rodman submitted plans to the Chief of Ordnance comprehending ten great shops, in two rows of five shops each, those on the north being designated for the Armory and those on the south for the Arsenal. These plans were approved, and General Rodman began the execution of his mighty work. He lived to see his plans for the Arsenal materialize in the construction of two of the shops and the quarters for the commanding officer. At the request of the Chief of Ordnance, he was buried upon the Island, in a sightly spot set apart for that purpose, near the National Cemetery. There a modest shaft stands.

## GEN. DANIEL W. FLAGLER.

General Rodman's successor was another eminent soldier, one who had made a brilliant record in the Civil War, though much younger and of lower comparative rank. On recommendation of the Chief of Ordnance, Capt. D. W. Flagler, then on duty at Rock Island Arsenal, was assigned to the command of the post, June 15, 1871. He served until May, 1886, when he was sent to Frankford Arsenal, Philadelphia; a period of nearly fifteen years, or about half the constructive stage of the Arsenal. Captain Flagler fully comprehended the far-reaching scope of the work before him, and gave it the best years of his life. It became a part of him, and he was deeply attached to it. The plans, as he received them, were imperfect in the details compared with the elaborate plant that has grown from them, with the many changes and improvements that have been made. Inventions of practical value, resulting in conceded economy, were applied by him. The progress of construction was supplemented by the manufacture of stores for the army. The commandant proved that ordnance stores can be manufactured here and distributed to the army cheaper than they can be fabricated in the East and brought West. During this command eight shops were entirely built — the commanding officer's quarters, buildings for officers' quarters, the soldiers' barracks, post buildings, a complete system of sewers, the Moline bridge, roads, streets and avenues, the water-power wall, grading and ornamentation of grounds. During the fifteen years the Arsenal

MAJ. STANHOPE E. BLUNT.
Present Commandant Rock Island Arsenal.

was largely shaped and adapted to its purpose as we see it at this time.

General Flagler was born in New York, March 24, 1835. His father's grandfather, Simon Flagler, came from Holland in 1735, and settled near Poughkeepsie, New York, where his grandfather, John Flagler, was born. The general's father, Sylvester Flagler, was born near Albany, and settled on the Holland purchase in western New York. He was graduated from West Point, June 24, 1861, No. 5 in his class. His rank was second lieutenant, captain in 1863, major in 1874, lieutenant-colonel in 1881, colonel, and in 1891 brigadier-general and chief of ordnance. His retiring year is 1899. He was promoted several times for gallant service in

95

CAPT. O. B. MITCHAM.

battle, and likewise honorably mentioned. His range of service has been wide, and he participated in several battles and skirmishes of the Civil War. He was chief of ordnance, Army of the Potomac, in 1862 and 1863; engaged in the battles of Fredericksburg, Chancellorsville and Gettysburg. He has held commands at Augusta Arsenal, at Frankford and Watertown, aside from his long term at Rock Island. His wide experience in the Ordnance Department, his anticipation of events, his scientific acquaintance with modern arms and the distinguishing quality of always being ready have been of inestimable value.

### COL. THOMAS G. BAYLOR.

This officer, who had more than won his rank, whose gallant conduct is history, who had served at Watervliet, Fort Monroe, and on important boards, followed Colonel Flagler, June 2, 1886, and continued in command until December 1, 1888, when he was assigned to Frankford Arsenal, where he died, September 19, 1890. Colonel Baylor was born in Virginia, May 4, 1837, and graduated from the Military Academy, July, 1857.

### COL. JAMES W. WHITTEMORE.

The next commandant at Rock Island Arsenal was Colonel Whittemore, assigned in November, 1889, and continued until March 14, 1891, when he was relieved and granted leave of absence for one year, at the expiration of which he was sent to the United States powder depot, Dover, New Jersey. He served there until March, 1897, when he was assigned to Frankford Arsenal. Colonel Whittemore retires in 1900. He graduated from West Point in 1860, and his meritorious services have been deservedly recognized. His command at Rock Island Arsenal, like that of his successor, was comparatively brief.

### COL. A. R. BUFFINGTON.

Colonel Buffington took command February 26, 1892, and retained it until March 22, 1897, when he was assigned to the United States powder depot, where he is now serving. He is a Virginian, born in 1837. His

CAPT. W. S. PEIRCE.

retiring year is 1901. He served actively during the Civil War, was commandant at Watervliet, Indianapolis, Allegheny, Baton Rouge, Watertown, Detroit and other Arsenals. He was an inventor, and one who refused to accept private gain when he could be of service to his country. Colonel Buffington's name is intimately connected with the barbette disappearing gun carriage, so formidable for use in the seacoast defenses of the country. His command at Rock Island, though not long, was marked by new and important constructive work.

## MAJ. STANHOPE E. BLUNT.

The three distinctive stages of Rock Island Arsenal are those dealing with the plans, the construction and the operation, yet a clear separation is not possible, the one is so linked into the other. But with the first period General Rodman was eminently connected ; with the second and the beginning of the third, General Flagler, and with the third, during the first war the Arsenal was called upon for extraordinary service, Major Blunt. The present commandant was selected to operate the plant on an increasing scale of magnitude when hostilities were not imminent, but there is positive reason to believe that he met the emergency demands in a way to more than satisfy the War Department.

LIEUT. O. C. HORNEY.

Major Blunt is given more than ordinary prominence, for an officer of his rank, in the official publication known as "Records of Living Officers of the United States Army." He was born at the Boston Navy Yard, September 29, 1850, of distinguished parentage on both his father's and mother's side. He was graduated from the Oswego High School in 1868, and from West Point, June 14, 1872, standing No. 3 in his class. He was assigned to the 13th Infantry, at Fort Douglas, Utah, and served in northwestern Wyoming and the Yellowstone Park until March, 1874. He was promoted and placed in command at Fort Steele, Wyoming; of Medicine Bow ; and performed engineering duty in Colorado and New Mexico in one of Lieutenant Wheeler's exploring and surveying parties. He was transferred to the Ordnance Department November 1, 1874. He was stationed at Frankford Arsenal until August, 1876 ; at the Military Academy to August, 1880, acting as instructor in mathematics, ordnance and gunnery. He was promoted to captain August 24, 1880, the first of his class to reach that grade. He served as chief ordnance officer and inspector of rifle practice at Fort Snelling and at army headquarters at Washington to July, 1888, as inspector of rifle practice and as aid-de-camp to General Sheridan, with rank of lieutenant-colonel, and subsequently with

THE COMMANDANT'S OFFICE.

rank of colonel. During this period he was in charge of different army divisions and department rifle competitions, winning prizes and medals in several matches. He has been complimented in orders by Generals Sheridan, Terry and Schofield for services in connection with rifle practice, the last named saying of Captain Blunt: "His services in connection with the development of an effective system of rifle practice in the army have been of the highest importance, and his name will long be honorably connected with this great advance in the military service of the country." He was assistant at Springfield Armory from 1889 to 1894; at Watervliet Arsenal from September, 1894, to March, 1897. In the meanwhile he served on several important boards of officers.

His "Rifle and Carbine Firing," published in 1885, and "Firing Regulations for Small Arms," in 1889, both prepared by order of the Secretary of War, are the authorized guides for instruction in the army and in the national guard of the different States. Among his other writings are the article "Target Practice," 1886, in *Farrow's Military Encyclopedia;* "Modern Military Rifle," 1893, read before the International Congress of Engineers at Chicago; the article on "Small Arms," 1895, in *Johnson's Cyclopedia.*

March 25, 1897, Captain Blunt was assigned to the command of Rock Island Arsenal. His promotion to the rank of major was made July 7, 1898.

## TEMPORARY COMMANDANTS.

Between the relief of one commanding officer and the assumption of command by his authorized successor, Rock Island Arsenal has been commanded by the following officers by virtue of their rank, according to the customs and rules of the service :

Maj. John R. McGinness, from November 30, 1888, to November 17, 1889.

Capt. Marcus W. Lyon, from March 14, 1891, to February 26, 1892.

### ARSENAL OFFICERS.

Capt. Orin B. Mitcham, assistant at the Arsenal, is an officer of varied experience. He is a Virginian by birth ; was graduated from West Point, June 17, 1874, and promoted to be a second lieuten-

CORNELIUS J. BROWN.
Chief Clerk Commandant's Office since 1872.

ant in the 4th Regiment of Artillery. He served on garrison duty, Fort Canby, Washington, nearly two years preceding March 21, 1876. He was transferred to duty at the Artillery school at Fort Monroe, thence to garrison in South Carolina, at Washington Arsenal, and again at Fort Monroe. He was assistant instructor and professor of modern languages at the Military Academy; transferred to the Ordnance

ASSISTANT OFFICERS' ROOMS.

Department and promoted to be first lieutenant June 23, 1879. He was assistant at Rock Island Arsenal two years, from 1881 to November, 1883. For the following three years he served in Wyoming. He was again at West Point as assistant instructor in gunnery for nearly four years, until August 28, 1890. About that time he was promoted to be captain. He was

99

CIVIL ENGINEER W. OTTO GRONEN'S OFFICE.

assistant inspector of steel at the Midvale Works, Pennsylvania ; assistant at the Watervliet Arsenal, and came from there to Rock Island four years ago last August.

Capt. William S. Peirce is a native of Vermont, thirty-four years of age. He was graduated from West Point in June, 1888, and commissioned second lieutenant, 2d Artillery, serving with that regiment three and a half years at Fort Barrancas, Florida; Fort Warren, Boston Harbor, and Fort Riley, Kansas. January 15, 1892, he was appointed first lieutenant, Ordnance Department, and served at the gun factory, Watervliet Arsenal, for three years. His next station was the Proving Ground at Sandy Hook, New Jersey, and the period was two years, and his duties were connected with the testing of heavy guns, powders and high explosives. He was recorder of the board for testing rifled cannon. April 24, 1897, Lieutenant Peirce was ordered to Rock Island Arsenal, where he was assigned to the charge of the machine, equipment and blacksmith shops and foundry. July 7, 1898, he was promoted captain.

Lieut. Odus C. Horney was born at Lexington, Illinois, September 18, 1866. He was appointed to West Point from Ohio, and graduated from that academy June 12, 1891, receiving his appointment as second lieutenant of the 7th Infantry. He served with the regiment at Fort Logan, Colorado, from 1891 to 1893, being in command of Company E for nearly a year. He was appointed first lieutenant in the Ordnance Department May 2, 1894, and since June 19 of that year he has served at Rock Island Arsenal. He has had charge of the carpenter and harness shops and of the water-power improvements. He is now in command of a detachment of ordnance and hospital corps.

Lieut. Clarence C. Williams, a Georgian by birth, graduated from West Point with the class of '94. He was transferred to the Ordnance Department in 1895. Lieutenant Williams, who has been on duty in the Philippines, left there for Rock Island Arsenal on October 26.

GEORGE DURNIN,
Paymaster's clerk, struggling with three
thousand names just before pay day.

THE CIVIL STAFF.

Although the Arsenal is in charge of the Ordnance Department, and the commandant and associate officers are army men, the thousands of employes in the offices and shops are from civil life. Commandants, as has been shown, come and go, but many of these faithful civilians remain. Among them are :

W. Otto Gronen, who, in charge of the drawing and engineering office, has served under every commandant, beginning early in 1870.

Cornelius J. Brown, who has been chief clerk since 1872.

READY FOR FIRE.

CUBAN MACHETES.

(These weapons, which very evidently have seen service, were found in a shipment from the battlefields about Santiago received at Rock Island Arsenal. On the unsheathed machete to the left are cut the words "Troop C," on the second "J. C. Goodwin, Tempe, A. T. [Arizona Territory], U. S. A.," and on the third the initials "W. F. H.")

# REASONS FOR CONTINUED SUPPORT.

*Reasons strong and forcible.—Shakespeare.*

AT some length the arguments for a more liberal support of Rock Island Arsenal by Congress have been given in this book. They may be recapitulated here, not in the order of their force, perhaps, for that is not material, but essentially:

1. The location was selected after exhaustive examinations by army boards, and that a mistake was made has never been charged. All the original reasons for the site have been strengthened.

2. The location is not only central, but, on account of this, stores made here can be sent more quickly to their destination, whether that be north, south, east or west. This economy of time might easily be a very serious matter. The fact of the short hauling of freight in delivering the output is also economy of money.

3. The surrounding and contributing country for five hundred miles is not equaled in the world for fertility — for the production of breadstuffs. Hence, living nowhere in the United States can be cheaper.

GEN. NELSON A. MILES.

(The Commanding General of the United States Army has visited Rock Island Arsenal since his return from Cuba and Porto Rico. He expressed surprise and gratification at the extent and character of the work done there during the war with Spain.)

4. The transportation facilities not only include, directly and indirectly, the great railroads, but the Mississippi River washes the shores of Rock Island, and the western terminus of the Illinois and Mississippi Canal is only three miles to the southwest.

103

HUNDREDS OF SADDLES.

(Equipment used by Roosevelt's Rough Riders. Shipped to Rock Island Arsenal from Santiago, Cuba, for repairs and to be reissued.)

5. Coal, iron, lead, copper and other minerals used in the fabrication of stores and munitions are within easy reach ; likewise lumber and leather.

6. The largest water power in the country, Niagara alone excepted, is available, and a part of it is actually utilized.

7. The military reservation on which the Arsenal is located is owned by the Government, and it is the largest military post in the United States.

8. The Arsenal shops, now practically finished at a cost of nearly $7,000,000, are the most expensive, the most capacious and the best adapted to the intended uses of any in the country.

9. In the crisis of 1898 the Arsenal was conspicuously first in the variety and magnitude of its output.

10. In time of peace as well as in war Rock Island Arsenal is the largest depot in the country for the issue of supplies to the army.

11. The security from attack by a foreign enemy is as perfect as the Nation affords. The navy of no foe can reach it, nor is it possible for an army of invasion to approach it.

12. The records at the War Department show that the health of this post has been exceptional from the first. The excellent natural sanitary conditions have been supplemented by approved drainage systems. The climate is temperate.

13. The Arsenal is in the center of an industrial community upon which calls may be made at any time.

14. While nearly $9,000,000 has been expended in constructing the great shops, the water power and the bridges, all controlled by the Government, only $309,627 has been appropriated for machinery and shop fixtures. Because of this oversight, acres of floor space are idle, and work is done at a disadvantage.

15. A comparatively small present outlay would vastly add to the effectiveness of the Arsenal and the economy of operating it.

THE ARSENAL COAT OF ARMS.

# THE ILLINOIS AND MISSISSIPPI CANAL.

It is a fact too well known to require extended discussion, that water routes generally, when they come into competition with transportation by land, are the most efficient and certain regulators of freight charges known.

There is nothing so democratic as free waterways and highways constructed and maintained by the public for the people.—*Captain W. L. Marshall's Report, Chief of Engineers, U. S. A., June 21, 1890.*

THE reasons which have been and are presented in support of the construction of the Illinois and Mississippi Canal may be thus summarized:

1. Cheap transportation to the East is even more an absolute necessity to the Upper Mississippi Valley than is such transportation to the South. In the direction of securing the latter very much has been done. But the main arteries of commerce flow from the West to the East, and from the East to the West.

L. L. WHEELER.

(Engineer in direct charge of the building of the Illinois and Mississippi Canal, under Maj. W. L. Marshall, Corps of Engineers, U. S. A.)

2. It is the particular misfortune of the Upper Mississippi Valley that it has no share in the vast benefits which accrue to the lake region in the matter of competition and cheap transportation, secured through the use of a water route which has its westward terminus at Chicago and its eastern in New York Harbor. The potency of the competition in freight charges maintained by the water route of the lakes, the Erie Canal and Hudson River stands confessed.

3. The great gain to the entire region west of Chicago to result from the extension to the water-route competition and cheapness to which attention has been directed, may be approximately estimated on comparison of railroad freight charges on lines of commerce with which water routes of transportation come into competition and those on which no such competition is known.

4. The vast volume attained by the annual cereal product of the States directly tributary to the Upper Mississippi presents yet additional support to the plea for an all-water transportation route to the East.

5. The fact that the producers of the Northwest do and must increasingly look to the exportation of their cereals, provisions, dairy products and cattle, as

offering the surest market and the largest profit, has also great weight in the argument urged in behalf of the Hennepin Canal.

6. Scarcely less important to the Upper Mississippi Valley region than the export of its products, rendered possible and profitable only when cheap transportation is secured, is the ready and inexpensive delivery of its imports. The aggregate of these increases year by year, while it has already reached proportion and value which are literally immense.

7. It is essential to a correct understanding of the demand for the completion of the Illinois and Mississippi Canal that the fact be fully comprehended that Chicago is the natural and the inevitable center of the commerce of the entire Northwest.

8. During the past few years there has resulted a radical change in the methods of transporting cereals. Grain is no longer sacked for shipment. Instead, it is carried in bulk from the various points in Minnesota, Wisconsin and Iowa on the Upper Mississippi ; the grain is

A SECTION OF THE CANAL READY FOR WATER.

oaded into barges in bulk, and in them floated down to railroad elevators, there to be transferred to railroad cars and carried to Chicago, or moved farther down the river to St. Louis, there to be transferred to larger barges, and in these carried to New Orleans. What is needed, then, is that grain-laden barges shall be enabled to float from any Mississippi River point direct to Chicago just as originally placed in cargo.

9. It is not pretended by any intelligent advocate of the Illinois and Mississippi Canal that it will or can compete with the railroads in the transportation of light freights or perishable goods.

10. So rapidly are increasing the yearly products of the Northwest that, as is well known to shippers and business men generally, it has already become a serious question, during the periods in which grain and stock are being pressed forward to market, whether the limits of capacity in railroad freight transportation have not been nearly reached.

ILLINOIS AND MISSISSIPPI CANAL.
(Lock 36, second above the Mississippi River.)

11. The railroads cannot possibly carry bulky and heavy freights as cheaply as these can be transported on canal, river and lake. This is as true as to the railroads which have been made the recipients of generous aid from the General Government, through grants of public lands — which in themselves would today constitute a princely domain — as it is of roads built wholly through the investment of private and corporate money.—*From an Argument by the late Edward Russell, appearing in the Report of the Chief of Engineers, U. S. A., 1883.*

The project under which the Illinois and Mississippi Canal is being built was reported upon in 1890, and the total estimated cost as given in that report is $6,925,960. The report of 1890 was based upon incomplete surveys, and more detailed surveys have made several important changes in the project which may materially change the cost of construction.

The primary object of this work is to provide a navigable waterway from the Upper Mississippi River to the Upper Illinois River, and in conjunction with the Illinois River and the Illinois and Michigan Canal, to furnish a short waterway from the Upper Mississippi River to Lake Michigan.

The present distance from Rock Island Arsenal to Chicago by water is 610 miles. When this canal is completed the distance will be reduced to 190 miles, a saving of 420 miles from all points on the Mississippi River above the Arsenal.

The summit level of the canal is 196 feet above the Illinois River where the canal enters it, and 96 feet above the Mississippi River at the mouth of Rock River. These differences of level are overcome by twenty-one locks on the eastern slope and by ten locks on the western slope. In addition, one guard lock is required on the western section and one on the feeder, making a total of thirty-three locks. The locks have chambers 35 feet wide and 170 feet long, and provide a depth of seven feet over the miter sills.

The amounts appropriated by Congress for this work are as follows:

| | | |
|---|---|---:|
| In 1890, | | $   500,000 |
| In 1892, | | 500,000 |
| In 1894, | | 190,000 |
| In 1896, | | 45,000 |
| In 1897, | | 875,000 |
| In 1898, | | 1,427,740 |
| | Total, | $3,537,740 |

The estimated amount required to complete the canal is $3,388,220.

With the money appropriated five miles of canal at the western or Mississippi River end were built, and have been in operation since April, 1895. This part of the canal enables boats to enter Rock River above the lower rapids and gives access to eight miles of river navigation which forms part of the main canal line. Several coal mines are reached from this part of Rock River, and the coal from them now finds a market along the Mississippi River.

On the eastern section of the canal route the earthwork for sixteen miles is finished and work is in progress over eight additional miles. The drainage structures for twenty-four miles are built and the masonry for twenty-one locks practically completed.

SHOWING SLUICE GATES AND LOCK 35.

CANAL GATES FROM FLOOR OF LOCK.

A STEAMER WITH TOW — IN THE CANAL.

On the feeder the entire right of way has been secured and is now being fenced. Contracts for eight miles of earthwork have been let, and it is expected that the whole feeder will be under contract by June 30, 1899.

On the western section, in addition to the five miles already in use, the right of way for sixteen miles has been secured and all necessary lands described.

The most detailed description of the Illinois and Mississippi Canal, however, will not give the reader so distinct an impression as the excellent and accurate map to be found elsewhere in this book. This map was reproduced from a much larger one, specially made under the direction of L. L. Wheeler, Assistant Engineer, in charge of field and construction work from the beginning. This map also shows correctly the location of Rock Island Arsenal, the surrounding cities, the railroad lines to the eastward, Rock River from its terminus to Dixon, Illinois—in fact, all the territory immediately tributary to the canal. Every mile of the waterway can be easily located and all distances can be computed.

A RAFTER PASSING ROCK ISLAND.

ROCK ISLAND — WHY SO CALLED.

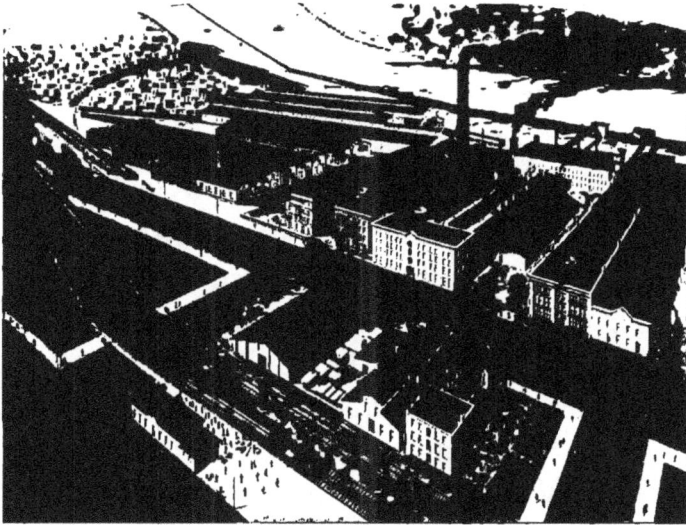

DEERE & COMPANY, MOLINE PLOW WORKS, MOLINE, ILL. ESTABLISHED 1847.

THE largest plant in the world for the manufacture of steel plows is that of Deere & Company, Moline, Illinois. Like many of our great manufacturing establishments, it had a very small beginning. Its foundation was laid when, back in 1837, John Deere, a pioneer from Vermont, began to construct by hand a few steel plows with which to tickle the prairies of Illinois. The first slab of plow steel rolled in the United States was made for him, and the present plant was established by him in Moline in 1847.

Very few years have passed since then that have not seen a material advance in the product of this concern, until now there is scarcely a civilized spot on the globe where agriculture is pursued that has not made the acquaintance of the John Deere Plows. Not only the prairies of Illinois but the whole face of mother earth has been turned from sadness into joy by their bright steel, and even desert places have been forced to yield abundant fruitage.

Already the largest steel plow factory in this or any country, the year of 1898 has seen some immense additions to the plant. A smith shop 150 by 266 feet, a grinding shop 100 by 266 feet, with annex nearly half as large, built entirely of steel and brick, with tile roofs, have been added, which nearly doubles the capacity of these departments of the works. These extensive improvements will lead to others in the near future. These additions are equipped with all modern conveniences for the economical handling of material, and are the most complete and modern shops of their kind to be found anywhere in this country.

The product of this factory consists of steel plows of all descriptions, harrows and cultivators, the annual output averaging over 150,000 complete implements.

Dealers in all parts of the country and in foreign lands are glad to handle them, as John Deere Plows are the acknowledged standard of the world in this line of manufacture, and the product of this establishment never goes begging for purchasers.

THE water power described in "Rock Island Arsenal: In Peace and in War" that is not used by the Government is used for generating ELECTRICITY for LIGHT, HEAT and POWER purposes and supplied to the consumers of this community in units from one-sixteenth to one thousand horse-power.

"Electricity is Life." If in need of additional life, apply to the

## Peoples Power Company,

ROCK ISLAND and MOLINE, ILL.

## Peoples Light Company,

DAVENPORT, IOWA.

CITY HALL, DAVENPORT.

xxxv

xxxvi

xxxvii

xxxviii

MOLINE PUBLIC HOSPITAL.

xxxix

xl

SCOTT COUNTY COURTHOUSE, DAVENPORT, IOWA.

xli

ARMORY HALL, ROCK ISLAND.

xliii

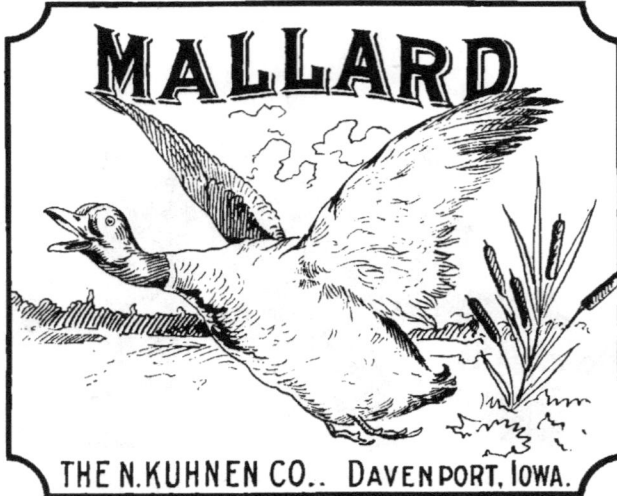

xliv

UNITARIAN CHURCH, MOLINE.

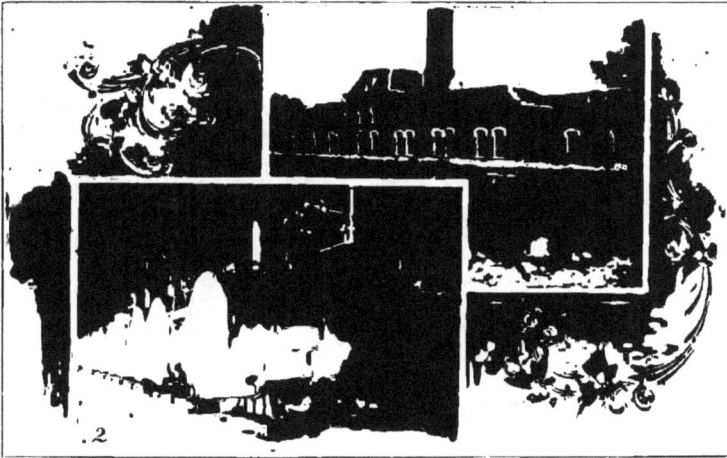

xlvii

xlviii

LINCOLN SCHOOL BUILDING, ROCK ISLAND.

xlix

# Rock Island Lumber and Manufacturing Co.

## ROCK ISLAND, ILL.

F. C. A. DENKMANN, Pres.                         J. P. WEYERHAEUSER, Sec. & Treasurer
H.   Vice Prest & Mang.                           R. C. IMSE

## SASH AND DOOR WORKS

ULDINGS, &c.

Rock Island, Ill.

CLARISSA C. COOK HOME FOR WOMEN, DAVENPORT.

# SYLVAN STEEL COMPANY,

## MOLINE, ILL.

G. WATSON FRENCH,
President.

NATHANIEL FRENCH,
Vice-President.

J. W. ATKINSON,
Secretary and
Treasurer.

G. H. TATNAL,
Superintendent.

———— *MANUFACTURERS* ————

**Merchant Bar and Refined Iron.     Hard and Soft Steel.**
**Agricultural Iron and Steel Shapes.**

---

# Deere & Mansur Co. MOLINE, ILL.

**CORN PLANTER WORKS.**

lv

The Entire Illustrative Contents of ROCK ISLAND ARSENAL IN PEACE AND IN WAR were ENGRAVED BY

A·ZEESE & CO

300-306 DEARBORN ST
CHICAGO
ILLINOIS

ESTIMATES and ROUGH SKETCHES CHEERFULLY FURNISHED ON APPLICATION

ENGRAVERS BY ALL PROCESSES

MASONIC TEMPLE, DAVENPORT.

lix

lxi

ST. PAUL AND MINNEAPOLIS
LIMITED EXPRESS
THE FINEST TRAIN IN THE WORLD
LEAVES CHICAGO DAILY AT 6.30 P.M.
Burlington Route
BEST LINE TO DENVER
Burlington Route
BEST LINE TO ST. PAUL AND MINNEAPOLIS
Burlington Route
BEST LINE TO OMAHA
Burlington Route
BEST LINE TO KANSAS CITY
Burlington Route
BEST LINE TO COUNCIL BLUFFS
Burlington Route
BEST LINE TO BLACK HILLS
Burlington Route
BEST LINE TO PUGET SOUND
Burlington Route
BEST LINE TO CALIFORNIA
Burlington Route
BEST LINE TO MONTANA
Burlington Route
BEST LINE TO TEXAS
PULLMAN BUFFET SMOKING CAR

# MERCY HOSPITAL, - - - Davenport, Iowa.

FRONT VIEW OF MAIN BUILDING.

THE NEW BUILDING.

The new addition to the hospital is especially arranged for the accommodation and comfort of surgical cases. Several suites of rooms are provided with private baths and adjoining rooms for private nurses or attendants. It is finished throughout with glass and tile, and contains all the modern apparatus necessary for the best surgical work.

SAENGERFEST HALL, DAVENPORT.

ILLINOIS WESTERN HOSPITAL — FRONT VIEW.
(Four miles east of Moline.)

Exterior View of Davenport Store.

WHITAKER BLOCK, CORNER THIRD AND BRADY STREETS, DAVENPORT.

# INDEX TO CONTENTS.

—

1.  THE NEW MODEL SPRINGFIELD.      2. FOR THE KRAG-JORGENSEN.

# INDEX TO ADVERTISEMENTS.

www.ingramcontent.com/pod-product-compliance
Lightning Source LLC
Chambersburg PA
CBHW020537270326
41927CB00006B/612